THE RELEVANT CHURCH

HE RELEVANT CHURCH

A New Vision for Communities of Faith

Edited by Jennifer Ashley with Mike Bickle, Mark Driscoll, Mike Howerton
and 12 More Leading Pastors

[RELEVANTBOOKS]

Published by Relevant Books
A division of Relevant Media Group, Inc.

www.relevantbooks.com
www.relevantmediagroup.com

© 2005 by Relevant Media Group

Design: Relevant Solutions
www.relevant-solutions.com

Interior design by Jeremy Kennedy
Cover design by Chuck Anderson

Relevant Books is a registered trademark of Relevant Media Group, Inc., and is registered in the U.S. Patent and Trademark Office.

For information or bulk orders:
RELEVANT MEDIA GROUP, INC.
100 SOUTH LAKE DESTINY DRIVE
SUITE 200
ORLANDO, FL 32810
321-206-8844

Library of Congress Control Number: 2004093614
International Standard Book Number: 0-9746942-4-X

05 06 07 9 8 7 6 5 4 3 2

Printed in the United States of America

REL·E·VANT

adj. 1. socially and culturally significant; important to real-world issues, present day events or the current state of society. 2. having a bearing on or connection with the matter at hand. 3. distinctive

REL·E·VANT CHURCH

n. 1. a distinctive community of faith that is passionate for Christ as well as culture. 2. a community of believers who has bearing on and significance in present day culture.

CONTENTS

INTRODUCTION

BY JENNY ASHLEY

A FEW YEARS AGO WHEN I WAS WORKING ON THE BOOK, *I AM RELEVANT,* I talked to a slew of people who were living out their faith in radical and unsuspecting ways. A cage-fighter with a passionate heart for God who focuses her energy on "being Christ" to her raucous, unbelieving teammates. A professional BMXer who views doing tricks on his bike as an act of worship. He even started a line of BMX clothing with Jesus-themed graphics because there was no presence of Christ in the BMX world.

But the more I talked to these essentially cool and brave Christians, the more I heard a similar mantra: No, I don't go to church. They may pray with their roommates and read the Bible on their own, but the concept of church had become completely irrelevant to their spiritual journeys. Was it because they were living out their faith in such an unforeseen, relevant way that people in the average church community (many of whom hide inside the "safe, Christian bubble") didn't know how to relate to them? Or possibly because they were judged for being immersed in such hard-edged facets of culture instead of shying away from them?

This kept me up at night. I kept thinking—there has to be churches where people like Casey and Rich could find genuine, passionate, and accepting Christian community. Essentially, I was asking, Where are all the cool churches?

So, I started doing some research. Asking around, diving into chat rooms, emailing pastors. And what I found was really eye opening. I found out that there are not only "cool" churches, but that people like me—in their twenties, who don't shy away from culture and love Christ with all their hearts—are gathering together worldwide in some radical, unsuspecting places. There are churches in skate parks where people are getting on their boards and worshiping God. Churches in teahouses and nightclubs. There are hip-hop churches where the pastor raps and break dances during the service. There are prayer rooms in pubs, contemplative services in art galleries. The list went on and on. And I couldn't stop telling people. I was so excited to find out I was part of a movement of passionate believers who were discovering Christ in a whole new version of church.

So, that's where this book comes in. If you're like twenty-five-year-old Renee, one person I talked with who was thrown out of leadership for dying her hair blue and hasn't stepped back into a church since, that is not the end of the story. The Church—the Body of Christ—is a living, breathing, changing community, and you are a part of it. It offers you love, security, challenge, significance, and acceptance. You just have to be brave and engage.

And for those of you like me who are encouraged to find out how people our age are worshiping Christ in vibrant new communities, in young churches that are relevant to twentysomethings everywhere from East L.A. to England—this book is for you.

And finally for the pastor, for the leader, for those who want to influence and encourage my generation to engage in culture and in church, continue to do so. We need you. You'll find that this collection of essays tosses a little anarchy into the discussion of what it means to be relevant. The writing is funny and irreverent, as well as encouraging and motivating. Reading each pastor's first-hand account of starting a new community of faith over the last few years—whether it be an experimental, creative arts church, or an urban missional community—will definitely challenge you to rethink the confines of church like no other book has. The unique and sometimes contrary perspective of each writer offers layered, surprising answers to the question of what it means to be relevant to this generation.

Thank you to each of the pastors who took the time to share their stories and ideas in this project. I am grateful to each of you, and I pray God uses this book for His glory—to surprise and enlighten all of us to just how big His Church really is.

THE PLAYERS:

AN **INTRODUCTION** TO THE AUTHORS

This book is a collection of essays and stories of young pastors and visionaries—all of whom have started vibrant communities where twentysomethings are gathering for worship. Some of the churches are brand new, just a few months old, while others have been going strong for almost a decade—but in the big scheme of church history, they are all newbies, still changing, experimenting, and making it their focus to stay immersed in culture, to be relevant to believers and skeptics alike.

"THE TRADITIONALIST"
BRIAN KAY
San Luis Obispo, California

Brian Kay may be a traditionalist and a die-hard Calvinist, but this guy makes age-old creeds and confessions relevant to his congregation every week by re-explaining their purposes. His grounded, pragmatic teaching style attracts academics, thinkers, students, and philosophers—both believing and not. In "The Local Church: Sometimes Annoying, But Never Optional," Brian admits that the local church may not be the most hip-looking place, but that being in a community of believers is essential and what we are created for.

"THE CONSPIRATOR"

ALEX MCMANUS

Los Angeles, California

At the very forefront of the experimental, urban church movement, Alex McManus sees himself and his brother Pastor Erwin McManus of Mosaic as co-conspirators with Christ. Working in the highly creative, highly diversified city of Los Angeles, Alex urges us to envision the faceted mosaic—that is, the many-pieced beauty—of the future Church. His essay, "Is Church Still Relevant?" offers some astounding answers and calls us to a global vision of the Church which belongs to the nations.

"THE SCREWBALL"

MARK DRISCOLL

Seattle, Washington

Mark Driscoll is hilarious. With self-deprecating, raw, and sometimes cocky humor, Mark Driscoll is that screwball from grade school who sat in the back of the class and drew pictures of the principal with a Mohawk. In "The Last of the Hepcat Churches," Mark tells his unlikely story of starting one of the leading emerging churches that has grown to more than two thousand members in less than a decade, Mars Hill Church in Seattle.

"THE PIXIE"

SANDRA BARRETT

Portland, Oregon

With good-natured love for young people, I imagine Sandra Barrett as an adorable glitter fairy, sprinkling our generation with vision and hope. In "Worship in the Skatepark," she tells the story of her good friends, the legendary Paul Anderson and Clint Bidelman—free-style competitors from the '80s who started SKATE-CHURCH a decade ago.

"THE VISIONARY"
IAN NICHOLSON
Surrey, England
As one of the visionaries who started the 24-7 Prayer movement alongside Pete Greig in England just five years ago, Ian Nicholson tells the amazing story of a group of faithful nobodies, who through no ambition of their own, fortuitously started a worldwide prayer movement in "Dreaming Up Outrageous Schemes With God."

"THE KINGPIN"
TOMMY KYLLONEN (a.k.a. Urban D.)
Tampa, Florida
In "Two Turntables and a Microphone," Tommy Kyllonen tells how his grassroots hip-hop youth ministry expanded to meet the needs of an entire congregation when Crossover Community Church needed a full-time pastor. Suddenly the kingpin, Tommy kept his focus on presenting the Gospel in a relevant way to a hip-hop culture.

"THE CAPO"
MIKE BICKLE
Kansas City, Missouri
In "Come to the Bridegroom," Mike Bickle unveils how he was transformed from a spiritually bored believer into a lovesick worshiper of God. With a call for young people to encounter the Bridegroom God—that is, a God who is fiery in His affections for you—Mike reveals how this generation is discovering how to be fascinated with God through disciplined intercession, which countless twentysomethings are experiencing in the prayer and healing rooms of the International House of Prayer.

"THE REALIST"
TIM KEEL
Kansas City, Missouri
Wanting to start a church for people who don't like church, Tim Keel created Jacob's Well in 1999. With a refreshing perspective and realistic considerations, Tim explains why now he actually loves church and the journey that took him there in "Love is of the Essence."

"THE BOHEMIAN"
KAREN WARD
Seattle, Washington
Known for hosting bohemians and artists in her tea house/church without a church, Karen Ward is the pastor of a missional community in the quirky urban Seattle neighborhood of Fremont. In "The New Church: Artistic, Monastic, and Commute-Free," Karen tells how she united her separate worlds of church and friends by creating a new community that was relevant to both.

"THE STRAIGHT-EDGE"
TODD SPITZER
Berkeley, California
A purist with an attitude, Todd Spitzer lays the smack down in "The Death of Cool," urging us to stop trying so hard to keep up with the latest ministry trends and offer people what they were made for: intimacy with Christ, only found by digging the ancient wells of Scripture. Through incredible stories and caustic humor, Todd reveals how a diverse mix of people at Regeneration Berkeley are being transformed by the beauty of Christ alone.

"THE ROCK STAR"
DUSTIN BAGBY
Manhattan, New York
My first impression of Dustin Bagby was that he was an actual rock star, but it turns out someday he just wants to be a chaplain for rock stars. I'd support that. In "God is in the Pub," Dustin describes how rather than sequester themselves inside a church building, he and his friends at Mosaic Manhattan spend more time in comedy clubs, pubs, and rock shows in order to be Christ to their urban community.

"THE ADVOCATE"
JASON ZAHARIADES
San Dimas, California
In "Being the Church vs. Going to Church," Jason Zahariades explains why he left full-time ministry to help start a small missional community in Southern California.

"THE MUSE"
HOLLY RANKIN ZAHER
Pittsburgh, Pennsylvania
In "Connect, Experience, Live," Holly Rankin Zaher tells the story of THREENAILS' first public gathering, a creative arts contemplative service held at night in an art gallery.

"THE MAVERICK"
MARK SCANDRETTE
San Francisco, California

Mark Scandrette is a free agent and rogue lover of Christ who moved to San Francisco to start a church but ended up forming a missional community comprised of his neighbors and friends—some are believers; others are not. In "A Week In the Life of a Missional Community," Mark shows us how we can create an integrated life of holistic worship—not just on Sundays or one night during the week. He challenges us to rethink the safe, often compartmentalized aspects of our Christian life and to start seeing our church community as every believer and potential believer with whom we are in relationship.

"THE GALLANT"
MIKE HOWERTON
Lake Forest, California

Sometimes young pastors that head up thriving, urban churches think they're too cool for school. Not Mike Howerton. Just about the nicest, most enthusiastic guy you'll find in the OC, Mike explains how young churches need to be not just purpose-driven, but first and foremost, value-driven in "The Value Driven Church," which details his vision for the college-age ministry at Saddleback Community Church.

01

THE LOCAL CHURCH:
SOMETIMES ANNOYING
NEVER OPTIONAL

BY BRIAN KAY

IT IS IMPOSSIBLE TO BE A FOLLOWER OF CHRIST AND NOT BE PART OF A LOCAL CHURCH. THERE, I SAID IT.

But I'm not the first. The early church father St. Cyprian put it even more offensively, "No one can have God as Father who does not also have the church as Mother."[1] Is there a degree of hyperbole to such claims? Yes. Are there exceptions to the rule? Of course. However, there are several good reasons to believe that the normal Christian life becomes entirely undone when it is not lived in the presence of other believers, in regular acts of worship and service.

The design of this chapter is to explain why someone like Cyprian could be so sure of his claim, as well as to explore what it really means to "go to church." In fairness, I should admit from the beginning that I am a pastor of one such local church, and probably stand something to gain if anybody decides to come. However, because some of what I say may be accused (wrongly, I think) of knee-jerk traditionalism, it might help to know that in my case, holding strong theological convictions about the Church does not amount to old-fashioned "churchiness" in the worst that that word connotes. For example, while I believe in the Church, I think Sunday school is over-rated, and when it comes to private taste, eight times out of ten, I cue up The Ramones over Bach. To say that church is necessary does not mean that any one given manifestation of church culture is necessary.

"THERE ARE SEVERAL GOOD REASONS TO BELIEVE THAT THE NORMAL CHRISTIAN LIFE BECOMES ENTIRELY UNDONE WHEN IT IS NOT LIVED IN THE PRESENCE OF OTHER BELIEVERS, IN REGULAR ACTS OF WORSHIP AND SERVICE."

When defining the Church, I tend to defer to the Reformers, who themselves deferred to Scripture. A local church is a group of professed believers in Jesus Christ (and their baptized children) who gather at least weekly to worship in song and prayer, partake in the Lord's Supper, and hear Christ preached from the Scriptures. As a covenantal community, church members publicly vow to serve one another and to be accountable to the elected elders in matters of doctrine and purity of living. If at least something like this is in mind when we speak of the local church, then "going to church" in its fullest sense means participating regularly in gathered worship and committing oneself to some degree of significant involvement in the lives of others in that congregation. It's hard to read the pastoral epistles (1 and 2 Timothy, Titus) without this rough portrait of early church life coming into focus. Such a church body becomes a visible counter-culture—not just some kind of ad hoc gathering—a functioning community of potentially otherwise disparate people known for its mutual love and shared conviction that Jesus Christ is the Lord of the universe and hope of the world.

"TO SAY THAT CHURCH IS NECESSARY DOES NOT MEAN THAT ANY ONE GIVEN MANIFESTATION OF CHURCH CULTURE IS NECESSARY."

But why not just worship and pray privately? For one reason or another, many who profess faith in Christ have been so frustrated or uninspired by the local churches around them that they live their Christian lives outside a committed fellowship to other believers. While some give up on the local church altogether, others go from church to church in an effort to put together a smorgasbord of the best teaching, best music, best small group, best whatever. Church hopping is the only tolerated promiscuity in Christian culture—enjoying temporary benefits of life in one worshiping community, then another, but without any formal obligation to settle down and serve in any.

The nature of the Gospel itself, though, ought to predispose us to join up with other believers. Christians are people who have come to Jesus Christ "the living stone" and then by virtue of His life become living stones themselves (1 Peter 2:4–5). They are then "joined together" by God as He builds His own spiritual house. An individual Christian therefore is part of a God-built structure made up of other believers in order to become a dwelling place for the Holy Spirit. Obviously, a stone that remains by itself doesn't make for much of a temple. While it is certainly true that individual believers have the Spirit of God dwelling in them personally, most of the New Testament language of indwelling is reserved for God's presence in the community of Christians—in short, churches. These days, a lot of nebulous talk about Christian community is passed around, and much of it is probably helpful in its own way. But at its core, the Christian community implied by 1 Peter 2 and many other passages is primarily a worshiping community that serves its members in various ways. Community in this theologically rich sense therefore is not what happens in big stadium rallies, movie chat-nights, volleyball games, or even Bible studies (as much as these things might flow from and support such community). Rather, Christian community is first a community of public worship, where the "spiritual house" gets put to use as the priests come together to offer "sacrifices acceptable to God through Jesus Christ." The people of God are defined as those who together "proclaim the excellencies of him who called you out of darkness into his marvelous light" (1 Peter 2:9). The future vision of the glorified Christian from the book of Revelation is really a vision of a glorified community of Christians, saints who stand shoulder-to-shoulder as they sing to the enthroned Lamb. If this is the destiny of individual Christians in the Church triumphant, it is natural to think that the Church militant—that is, today's Christians—would also regularly gather for the same purpose.

But worship is not the only mark of the Church. If it were, then casually gathering with friends to sing or read the Scriptures aloud would constitute full-bodied church life. The New Testament portrait is richer and more demanding. Since true worshipers are glorifying a Jesus Christ who served them through His death, they naturally seek to pour out their own lives in service of each other. This is a simple reflex: If Christ loved His people enough to profoundly suffer for them, me included, how can I not be concerned about those people whom my Savior Himself loves (even if they're older than me, younger, annoying, or culturally different)? Certainly we ought to love all people, non-Christians included, by virtue of their being in the image of God, but we give a legitimate priority to the other "living stones," to worshipers of the risen Jesus. Paul says, "Do good to all men, especially those of the household of faith" (Galatians 6:10). Serving the physical/emotional/social needs of fellow-worshipers with the same energy that we serve our own is a goal of the normative Christian life; it does not appear to be optional for those who happen to be "joiners." Try this experiment: Even if you disagree with me, entertain for a moment the idea that a Christian is someone who by definition is always gathering with others to worship, and always serving those with whom he worships. Now, read Acts, Romans, and 1 Corinthians. If you're like me, behind every bush, you'll see corporate worship and service as the routine habits of those whose basic instincts Christ has so fundamentally changed. How do you live out group worship and personal involvement with other Christians as a way of life? No one's come up with a better way than the oldest of old-school answers: Join a local church.

"THE CHURCH WILL BE MOST PROVOCATIVE AND ALLURING WHEN IT IS BEING ITSELF, BEING WHO GOD HAS CONSTITUTED IT TO BE, THAT IS, BEING A MINI-SOCIETY THAT PROCLAIMS THE PERSON AND WORK OF CHRIST, AND IMITATES HIS SACRIFICIAL SERVICE."

If any of this seems overly critical of churchless Christians, I admit that my own guild ironically deserves blame for keeping people away from its congregations. My private theory has been that many young people avoid churches these days because they sense a creeping cheesiness in the very way churches try to appeal to them. As twentysomething Sarah Hinkley wrote in *First Things* magazine, "We know you've tried to get us to church. That's part of the problem. Many of your appeals have been carefully calculated for success, and that turns our collective stomach."[2] Since the 1970s, many American pastors began to turn to the experts of the "church-growth movement" who told them the best way to reach people who thought the Church was irrelevant was to appeal to something that is undeniably relevant to the mass culture: being entertained. Sermons got wittier, music lyrics got catchier, and meat-and-potatoes theology took a back seat to just about everything else. A famous pastor in Orange County openly refused to talk about sin from the pulpit on the grounds that it was a turn-off to people with shaky self-esteem. The appeal of Christianity seemed to become: "Jesus is fun! Hey, come on, give Him a try!" In a way, the church-growth movement worked, because a lot more people started coming on Sunday. But, as its music and preaching became more trivial, many other sensible people stopped taking the Church seriously. Who could blame them? The mode of church life they witnessed, even in cases where the doctrine was solid, was pure mayonnaise. And as the saying goes, no one will take the Church seriously until the Church starts taking itself seriously.

"WHEN SUNDAY IS FIRST ABOUT FEEDING ON CHRIST AND HIM CRUCIFIED, MOST PEOPLE WON'T FEEL SO STARVED, EVEN IF EVERYTHING ELSE ABOUT THE CHURCH IS LESS POLISHED, AND NEITHER WILL YOU."

What's to be done? Churches need to remember one of the basic phenomena of human attraction: The least likable kid on the playground was always the one trying hardest to be liked. The cool kids, on the other hand, were popular partly because they didn't seem to care if they were liked; they were doing their thing whether or not you were watching. Those were the kids the rest of us openly (or secretly) admired (or envied). The theological version of this grade-school truism is that the Church will be most provocative and alluring when it is being itself, being who God has constituted it to be, that is, being a mini-society that proclaims the Person and work of Christ, and imitates His sacrificial service. The Church will be least relevant when it is caught in the act of reinventing itself to gain more friends. I remember as a teenager that the surest way to get me to avoid a Christian youth event was to show me a flier promising "cool music and awesome teaching." That meant that for sure the music wouldn't be cool, and the speaker would be more aware of himself, or me, than of God.

The challenge facing aesthetically and theologically sensitive Christians is that while many churches seem under-awed at the beauty and majesty of God and His Gospel, our Lord does not give us the privilege of sitting out from congregational life (Hebrews 10:25). The real question therefore is how to find a church that takes itself and its mandate seriously. Most postmoderns have too long a list of criteria, which is why they are rarely satisfied in any one congregation long enough to stay. Let me then suggest just one test, which I have found to be a great overall predictor of a church's character of ministry. If a church passes this test, a lot of other weaknesses it may have are worth putting up with, or staying around long enough to help change. This is a question to be asked about the Sunday preaching, and a question I try to apply to myself every week: Did Jesus Christ need to die on the cross for this message to be preached? That is, is the theme of any sermon controlled by the redeeming work of Jesus for me and outside of me more than it is by what I should do for Him or for others (as linked as both ideas must be)? In my experience, when God's work for us—through Christ's life, death, resurrection, and intercession—is more the focus than our emotional response, behavioral changes, whatever, then worship and community have the way paved before them. Other weaknesses in our programs and music, real or perceived, are relativized in peoples' minds. When Sunday is first about feeding on Christ and Him crucified, most people won't feel so starved, even if everything else about the Church is less polished, and neither will you. Churches like this exist, and often they aren't very sexy. Advice from a modern fan of Cyprian: Develop a taste for Christ-centered worship, find a church that shares that taste, and then join it.

1. St. Cyprian, De unit. 6: PL 4, 519
2. Sarah Hinkley, "Talking to Generation X," *First Things* 90 (February 1999) 10-11.

> " I DON'T THINK THERE IS ANY QUESTION IN SCRIPTURE THAT GOD EXPECTS US TO COME TOGETHER IN A COMMUNITY TO WORSHIP HIM AND SUPPORT EACH OTHER. THE THRUST OF THE NEW TESTAMENT FROM ACTS ONWARD IS ABOUT FOLLOWERS OF CHRIST RISKING THEIR LIVES AND FREEDOM TO MAKE BELIEVERS AND ESTABLISH CHURCHES. NOWHERE DOES PAUL OR SILAS OR PETER GO INTO A CITY TO MAKE BELIEVERS, THEN SEND THEM HOME AND EXPECT THEM TO SIMPLY PRAY BY THEMSELVES AND IN SO DOING FOLLOW CHRIST. "
>
> —ROBIN LEMKE
> SEATTLE, WASHINGTON, AGE TWENTY-NINE

CHAPTER ONE

IS THE 02 CHURCH STILL RELEVANT?

BY ALEX McMANUS

YOUNG AND JAPANESE, SHIHO WALKED INTO THE MIDST of an ethnically diverse crowd that gathered in a nightclub just west of downtown Los Angeles. An undergraduate student at UCLA, she exuded an aura of calm and warmth, and was supremely easy to like. Throughout the night, the twentysomething crowd sang together, listened to each other, gave hard-earned money, laughed from the belly, and hung out together until forced to leave. Shiho had just experienced a Mosaic gathering, a celebration of hope in Jesus Christ.

One of the things we always want to know is why people come to Mosaic (or church in general). Shiho's answer to this question warmed our hearts: "I wanted to be somewhere where God could find me." She became a regular at the Sunday night gatherings and soon became a follower of Jesus with us and an influencer among her peers. The question, "Is church still relevant?" has many answers today. Shiho's story reminds me that we should ask something further: For whom is church relevant?

When thinking about the relevance of church, the first question we must ask is whether or not church is still relevant to Jesus Christ.

Mike was a longhaired, soccer playing college dropout. A friend invited him to Mosaic. He and his girlfriend Beatrix, a fashion designer, soon became Christ followers. As a result of their conversion, they decided to pull back on the level of intimacy in their relationship and instead started to date. To my memory, they didn't even hold hands again until they married many months later. Individually and as a couple, these two brought their discipline, focus, and zeal to bear on others for the kingdom. Within a very short period of time, they were leading a small group community and eventually became regional small group overseers. Jesus not only found them; He began to bring many through them into kingdom community. If a community journeys with Jesus on His mission to find women and men, they will tend to be relevant to Jesus Christ.

"WHEN THINKING ABOUT THE RELEVANCE OF CHURCH, THE FIRST QUESTION WE MUST ASK IS WHETHER OR NOT CHURCH IS STILL RELEVANT TO JESUS CHRIST."

It was Mike and Beatrix who brought Shiho to Mosaic and to faith. Shiho and her dynamic boyfriend, Colin, also chose to change the nature of their relationship and followed a similar path as Mike and Beatrix. Today Colin and Shiho (now married) live in Seattle and are active participants in planting new churches (including a Mosaic in

Seattle), and Mike and Beatrix are leading the small groups at Mosaic Manhattan, a new church plant in New York City. None of this made the news. But their stories and a thousand other stories like them are how the world is being changed for the better all around us.

"THE OTHER QUESTION TO ASK IS, IS CHURCH RELEVANT TO THE FUTURE? THE FUTURE IS A MOSAIC—THE FUTURE IS BROWN. THE FUTURE IS PLURAL. THE FUTURE IS SPIRITUAL. THE FUTURE IS URBAN. THE FUTURE IS VIOLENT. AND THE FUTURE IS HERE."

Mike, Beatrix, Shiho, and Colin are all co-conspirators with Christ and are living lives that are relevant to the kingdom. When I have them in mind, I think yes, the Church is relevant to both Jesus and those who, like Shiho, wonder if God can find them.

Beyond being relevant to Jesus, the second thing we must ask is, "Is church relevant to outsiders?" Many of the contemporary churches (a.k.a. the classic baby boomer churches of the '80s) are still relevant in 2004 specifically for baby boomers. Many of the newer emerging churches are relevant for today's twentysomething Christians who don't like contemporary churches. But what about the person who isn't reacting against traditional or contemporary churches? What about the person who isn't shopping for the church that is right for them? What about the person who is looking for more than just an enhanced experience? What about the person who, like Shiho, wonders if God can find them? Is church relevant to them?

The scriptures tell us it is not good for man to be alone. This truth has application beyond marriage. People are designed for relationships and for community. God Himself lives in a relationship of love between Father, Son, and Spirit. And we are created in His image. Living in community is in the human genome. The need to belong is a human need (not just a Christian need), and as long as there are humans, communities of faith that are on a mission with Christ to reach and

include others will tend toward relevance. Moreover, outsiders themselves will feel a tug in the heart toward communities that are rich in
hope, love, and faith. That is how the soul is crafted.

Beyond being relevant to Jesus and to outsiders, the third thing we
must ask is, "Is church relevant to the future?" I believe the future is a
mosaic, and it happened yesterday. The future is brown. The future is
plural. The future is spiritual. The future is urban. The future is violent.
The future is here.

"CREATIVITY IS ONE OF THE EVIDENCES THAT WE ARE NOT ROBOTS SUBJECT TO AN UNCHANGEABLE FLOW OF EVENTS. IT IS PROOF OF THE FREEDOM OF THE HUMAN SPIRIT."

Well over a decade ago, *Time* magazine published a special edition
titled, "The New Face of America." The cover was a computer-gen-
erated face that integrated the features of a variety of ethnicities.
The face was beautiful. The face was brown. The face looked like my
Brazilian wife.

The future will feature not just many ethnicities in one community,
but many ethnicities in one family, and even in one person. For example, what ethnicity is Tiger Woods? This new ethnic plurality may
open exciting new ways for thinking about interracial relations. I tell
my children they have the blood of three continents (South/Cen-
tral America, Europe, and Africa) flowing through their veins. Love
everybody. In the same manner, our spiritual conversations won't only
be with Hindus or Muslims or Jews, but will also be with individuals
who hold a hodgepodge of beliefs. This plurality of human identity
will place front and forward the creative communication through
multiple and diverse media of the story of Christ. The future is plural.

The future will depend on creativity. One of Mosaic's core values is "Creativity is the natural result of spirituality." Spirituality and creativity are not the captives of an elite few, but are the birthright of all. Creativity is one of the evidences that we are not robots subject to an unchangeable flow of events. It is proof of the freedom of the human spirit. Our hope for the human future lies in our ability to think and act in new ways. Creativity is a universally human point of connection with both each other and God. The future is spiritual.

The future is urban. The Church in America has relocated to the suburbs, while at the same time, God has been urbanizing the world. The global church (in Korea, Peru, Brazil, El Salvador, Cairo, etc.) has demonstrated that churches can reach the cities in a big way, though some of these churches may now be struggling to maintain their relevance. The Church in America has learned how to capture the suburban migration of the Church. Now we must turn to the cities.

The future is violent. After 9-11, many of us were hesitant to send out international teams or even to fly domestically. At Mosaic, we've come to understand through the decades that the future (not just the cities) is violent, and we should get used to living in a world that is continually or regularly on a high alert status.

Communities of faith that desire to be relevant will need to be able to swim in the waters of this future mosaic. And because this future is here, I can encourage you with confidence: Christ following communities can indeed swim these waters and swim them well.

Mosaic is a community of faith that inhabits the city of Los Angeles and surrounding areas. Presently, we meet in four different locations, none of which we own. Our longest standing location is just west of downtown in a nightclub formerly owned by Prince. Our newest location is the Beverly Hills High School. I cannot tell you where we'll be meeting next year. Mosaic thrives in the midst of a diverse city in a diversity of locations.

More than fifty nationalities are represented in Mosaic's community of faith. We're nearly 40 percent Asian, 30 percent Latin, and 30 percent Caucasian, African-American, Middle Eastern, and other. Between our eldership and our leadership team meetings, we'll account for a large chunk of the world with representations of the Japanese, Chinese, Mexican, African, El Salvadorian, Italian, and Brazilian. And yes, we even have some fair skinned blonds in the mix.

The average age of our church is around twenty-five years old. Eighty-two percent are single. *The Los Angeles Times* described Mosaic as housing the largest concentration of artists in the Southland. On any given Sunday, guests could expect to see dance, original theater, original music, original short films, sketch comedy, and sculptors and/ or other artists creating a piece during the celebration. Sure, you say, that's L.A. But lamentably, most churches here are not filled with this kind of worshipful expression. Most churches here are just like most churches where you are—not diverse but homogenous, not creative but routine, not youthful but dying out.

"MOSIAC EXISTS NEITHER TO GROW AS LARGE AS WE CAN WITH SUBURBAN BELIEVERS NOR TO CREATE THE BEST EXPERIENCE FOR BELIEVERS WHO NEED SOMETHING A LITTLE MORE 'HIP.'"

If I had to put my finger on why Mosaic thrives in the brown, plural, spiritual, and violent city of L.A., I would say it is because it is consumed by God's love for the nations. This is not a guarantee, just a guess. We've been conspirators for Christ on international soil approaching three decades now. At present, we have approximately fifty adults from our community advancing the kingdom overseas. Our love for the nations has led some of us to take undercover assignments in some of the most dangerous parts of the world for the cause of Christ. This love compels us to call others to live with the death and victory of Christ near to the heart. This love has convinced us that there is no such thing as missions. There is only mission—the flaming center of what Jesus is about for the whole Church in the whole world throughout all of history. Even in America. Even today.

This love for the nations expresses itself at Mosaic as a kind of clandestine revolution, and it has been this way for a long time. So in a very real sense, we are not a contemporary church (e.g., the '80s suburban family church), and neither are we an emerging church (some of which focus their energy solely on being the new thing, under the assumption that new is always better). We are part of a global insurrection instigated by Jesus, an experimental church that seeks to create a mosaic community that will bless the mosaic future.

First, my prayer for the traditional churches is, as they decrease, may Christ increase. Second, the fact that a church is new or emerging doesn't necessarily mean that it is relevant to Christ, outsiders, and the future. Lastly, many of the contemporary churches focus on reaching their generation. Many of the newer emerging churches also focus on reaching their generation of Christians who feel out of place in contemporary churches. Both of these clans are strong, like lion prides, and their strategies are fine for their audiences. We commend them to their work. I sometimes tell my brother, Erwin, that if the Christian movement were the *Lion King* movie, the contemporary churches and the emerging churches would be the strong lion prides. We (Mosaic) would have to be Rafiki, the baboon. They prowl the savannah. They rule. They hunt together. They are to be feared. On the other hand, we shake a coconut, throw some dust, do a little dance, and can't figure out how to cover our butts.

Our calling is different. We exist neither to grow as large as we can with suburban believers nor to create the best experience for believers who need something a little more "hip." We exist to follow Jesus on His mission to proclaim the good news to the nations. Our focus then on both the local and international levels tends toward the person who wonders if God can find them, the one who has no access to our treasure, for the purpose of taking this treasure to him in the brown, plural, spiritual, violent city. Welcome to the future.

> **" I THINK I DISCONNECT FROM THE GOSPEL OF JESUS CHRIST WHEN I'M NOT INVOLVED IN CLOSE RELATIONSHIPS WITH OTHER BELIEVERS. "**
>
> **— TYLER WATTS**
> RIVERSIDE, CALIFORNIA, AGE TWENTY-ONE

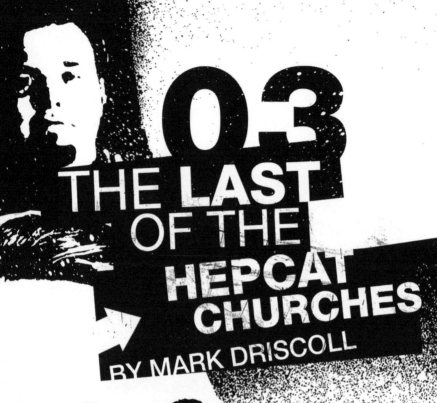

03
THE LAST OF THE OF THE HEPCAT CHURCHES

BY MARK DRISCOLL

WHEN I WAS YOUNG, I THOUGHT OUR LOCAL PRIEST WAS Jesus. He wore the same robe as Jesus in all the pictures they showed us in Sunday school. I was supposed to listen to everything he said. And every time I saw him, there were crowds gathered around him.

I grew up in the Catholic Church, the oldest of five children. We were a working-class Irish Catholic family, and as a child, I believed there was a God, and I prayed to Him in bed every night. But as I grew older, going to church seemed to lose its mystery and instead felt like a wearisome exercise routine for seniors—sit, stand, kneel, stand, sit, kneel, stand. And instead of our priest reminding me of Jesus, he seemed to be imitating the teacher from the Peanuts, wah wah wah-ing away as I was induced into a catatonic state of disinterest.

At some point in my teens, I continued to believe in something like God—a sort of nebulous Sky Fairy, but I hit the eject button on church and focused instead on being popular, playing baseball, and finding a girl to date who wasn't high maintenance. Occasionally I would drop in to church out of guilt or love for my concerned mother, but always walked away feeling as if I'd just wasted an hour with an ex-girlfriend.

Upon graduation from my public high school purgatory, I moved from Seattle to a rural college town and joined a fraternity in hopes of living like an intern at the Playboy Mansion. But, something strange happened—my conscience would not permit me to join the fool's parade of fellow hairy-backed image bearers in consuming cheap women and cheap beer. Even though I was no longer in the Church, I was surprised to discover that part of the Church was still in me and had shaped more of me than I had realized. To make matters worse, each day, I walked past a number of churches on my way to class, and something in me that plunged deeper than classic Catholic guilt caused me to question why I had been avoiding churches.

For the first time in my life, I was away from my family, my friends, even my girlfriend Grace. I was living as an independent adult and suddenly had this desire to come to my own conclusions about Jesus, the Bible, and church. Weary of the incessant whining about Christianity from my faux hippie professors in nearly every class, I decided to simply pick up the Bible for myself to see what it said, because until that point, I had gotten a lot of spirituality, morality, tradition, and stale communion wafers, but very little Scripture.

As I read the Bible, the primary themes that stuck out were that I suck and Jesus is God, but at some point, God gave me the faith to be a Christian. Subsequently, I began desiring to build friendships with other Christians. But, rather than joining a church, I connected with a collegiate parachurch ministry. The students who attended were primarily burned-out church kids living off the fumes of summer camp highs. Occasionally they would tell horrendous stories of their family church that were so disturbing, you'd think they stay awake at night shaking from post-tramautic stress syndrome. While the students in the ministry acted like a church, complete with weekly gatherings for Bible teaching and singing, they commonly critiqued churches and boasted that they were not a church. But, their declarations rang as hollow as a couple who had lived together for ten years, birthed three children, yet continually insisted that they were nothing like a married couple. After a few months in the ministry, I had made some good friendships, but grew weary of worshiping solely with people who were young, single, and theologically uninformed like me.

"OCCASIONALLY, I WOULD DROP IN TO CHURCH OUT OF GUILT, BUT ALWAYS WALKED AWAY FEELING AS IF I'D JUST WASTED AN HOUR WITH AN EX-GIRLFRIEND."

Simultaneously, I continued reading the Bible and kept seeing that the New Testament was written by pastors of churches to churches about church life. And, I was convicted that there is no such thing as a personal isolated relationship with Jesus apart from His often ugly bride, the Church. Acknowledging my disinterest in the Church as little more than arrogant judging, I decided to seek out a church where I could obey the Scriptures' commands to go to church (Hebrews 10:25), place myself under the authority of pastors (Hebrews 13:17), use my abilities to build up a church (1 Corinthians 14:12), partake of communion in a church (1 Corinthians 11:17-34), and give my tithe to a church (2 Corinthians 8-9). I was finally starting to realize Jesus died not just for me, but for His Church, which I was made a part of by His death and resurrection (Acts 20:28). I then had to decide where to go, which was a frightening prospect, because theologically I had become a Protestant, but had no idea how to distinguish between a good church and the kind of church where in the end everyone is standing around in shiny matching white shoes sipping on Kool-Aid.

I ended up in a church that had bland aesthetics, an unimpressive sound system, and mediocre worship leaders; yet what held it together was a godly Bible-centered pastor and a community of people from various stages of life and backgrounds, some of whom even reminded me of Jesus. My few years in that church are some of the richest in my life. My fondest memories of being in that church revolve around the small home of a very large family (eleven children today and counting). They often had my then fiancee Grace and I into their home to learn about the grace of God in marriage and parenting by allowing us to eat dinner at their table and sit on the couch to read to their children. After getting married and graduating from college, Grace and I left our college town, and unfortunately, that wonderful church. Our last stop on the way out of town was to say goodbye to the couple who had mentored us, and as we drove away, I could barely see the road through my tears as the children stood in the driveway waving goodbye and singing, "May God Bless You And Keep You" in von Trapp harmony.

"I WAS TWENTY-FIVE AND CERTAIN THAT MY CHURCH WOULD BE NEW, DIFFERENT, AND ESSENTIALLY COOL. I QUICKLY LEARNED THAT BEGINNING A CHURCH WAS FAR MORE DIFFICULT THAN CRITICIZING ONE."

When we got to Seattle, we began searching for a new church— which was devastatingly a lot like test-driving used cars in a junkyard and hoping to find one that at least runs. Finally, we found a large suburban church that was nearly an hour away from our home. And it was at that church where I got my first ministry experience as the college director and began seeing the inner workings of a large church from a front row seat—which at times was as shocking and disturbing as seeing yourself naked in a full length mirror ... from behind. In that experience, all my illusions about the Church being a simple and wonderful place evaporated. I realized that the Church is people and that people are sinful, and therefore churches are messy. After roughly two years at that truly very good church, I left to plant my own church, Mars Hill. I was twenty-five and certain that my church would be new, different, and essentially cool. I quickly learned that beginning a church was far more difficult than criticizing one, in the same way that cussing out the second baseman at a baseball game from the stands is easier than turning a double play on the field. In addition, our small church planting core of good people continually attracted the usual assortment of mixed nuts, from old legalists who wanted to argue about the King James Bible to a clan of hip urban creative garage band types who claimed to have a relationship with Jesus, but what that really meant was Jesus was one of their groupies.

On the opening night of our broke, young, disorganized church, I kicked out a heretic before climbing into the pulpit to preach my first sermon and ranted for nearly an hour about how we were going to be different and better than the other churches. And, in classic spoiled brat fashion, I likely blamed all the problems for the state of the Church on my parents' generation with predictable Woodstock protesting. After preaching, I sat in my seat to sing our depressing d-chord indie rock worship songs by candlelight with my congregation. Then, it dawned on me that in roughly ten to twenty years when I had gotten old, fat, and predictable, some young punk would likely be planting a church down the street from mine and kick things off by blaming me for ruining Christianity and taking my place until he too eventually became the old, fat, and predicable victim of the next young punk.

Simultaneously, the American evangelical Christian marketing beast was apparently starving for young fresh meat, because I soon got a phone call inviting me to speak at one of the first national conferences for young hepcat pastors that were starting new emerging churches. All of us innovative cutting edge culturally-relevant free-spirited nonconformists who curiously looked and sounded the same gathered to jump up and down making bold claims about how we were going to revive the Church and change the world in predictable high-fiving white guy fashion.

Since that time, the movement (if it can be called that) has gone pretty much like every other attempt to make the Church relevant to culture. Some of the hepcat churches failed and died for reasons varying from pastors who couldn't keep their fly up to simple burn out and exhaustion. Others have become small and negative by spending their time picking apart what other churches are doing rather than actually doing something, much like a music critic who makes a living critiquing bands, but who has never written a song.

"IN THE END, THE FUTURE OF THE CHURCH IS MUCH LIKE THE PAST AND PRESENT OF THE CHURCH—MESSY."

A few hepcat churches have become healthy, growing, and influential. Depending upon whom you speak to, my church (*www.marshillchurch. org*) is either one of these hepcat hothouses, or now yet another cop-out megachurch. The same can be said for the many churches our network of mainly young pastors have planted across the country and in other nations (*www.A29.org*).

In the end, the future of the Church is much like the past and present of the Church—messy. Churches that embrace their traditions over their children will die slow and painful deaths. Churches that embrace cultural relevance over biblical faithfulness will in time become heretics like Hymenaeus. The majority of small and struggling churches will cling on for dear life and keep reading books about the rapture in hopes that they can simply get out before they give up. And, God will put His hand on young punks who are unfit for the kingdom of heaven and fill them with a one-hundred proof shot of the Holy Spirit that transforms them from the typical Christian consumer or complainer into a co-laborer with Jesus who will remain busy building His Church just like He promised. These new pastors will plant new churches that attract new people with new questions that can only be answered by the old story that we're all sick and need Jesus.

" THE PHRASE 'GO TO CHURCH' MAKES ME CRAZY. I AM THE CHURCH. BELIEVERS ARE THE CHURCH. INSTEAD OF TALKING ABOUT JUST GOING INTO A BUILDING FOR A SERVICE, LET'S START TALKING ABOUT GETTING TOGETHER WITH OTHER BELIEVERS TO DISCUSS GOD AND PRAY TOGETHER. THAT TYPE OF GATHERING IS WHERE WE'LL FIND COMMUNITY, A PLACE OF ENCOURAGEMENT, SHARING, LISTENING, AND WORSHIP. **"**

—JEREMY WALDEN
AUBURN, ALABAMA, AGE THIRTY-ONE

WORSHIP IN THE SKATEPARK

BY SANDRA BARRETT

04

PAUL AND CLINT WERE INSEPARABLE FRIENDS IN junior high and high school. Growing up in the San Luis Obispo, California, skate culture of the '70s and early '80s, they were both chosen for the Central Coast Surfboards skate team and emerged as top freestyle competitors. But essentially, they were still just a pair of defiant skate rats—stealing wood to build ramps, trespassing to find a good run, drinking, getting high—it was a way of life.

But their junior year, things took a turn. Clint was invited to a church ski retreat and decided to go. Why? To hook up with a girl, of course. But that weekend, God made it clear to Clint that he was separated from God, a pretty frightening thought. He was gripped by his need for Christ and was amazed by the Gospel.

Months earlier, while Paul was partying at the beach, he heard a young Christian guy preaching at him through a bullhorn from the top of the embankment. That wasn't the first time he'd been faced with a challenge to rethink his lifestyle. He knew Jesus had him by the collar and wasn't about to let go. By seventeen, both Clint and Paul had given their hearts to Jesus and underwent a radical lifestyle change. Continuing to skate as sponsored amateurs, they both moved to Portland, Oregon, in 1987 and started school at Multnomah Bible College.

A few months later at the campus library, Paul was hitting the books, trying to prepare for an upcoming class. Spotting his skateboard, some local kids who were ditching the youth service at the nearby church made a beeline straight for him. Though he knew he should witness to them, he was annoyed instead since they were distracting him from his studies. So he told them they could take his board outside.

"THEY WERE JUST A PAIR OF DEFIANT SKATE RATS—STEALING WOOD TO BUILD RAMPS, TRESPASSING TO FIND A GOOD RUN, DRINKING, GETTING HIGH—IT WAS A WAY OF LIFE."

No idiot, he quickly realized that they were going to steal it. With that thought in mind, he pushed back from the table and went outside to talk to them.

The rest is skateboard history. From that day, Paul Anderson made it his mission to hang out with skaters and in his own way, become a "fisher of men." He felt for the kids because he knew they didn't fit in with local conservative youth groups. So when he wasn't in school, Paul spent his time with high school and junior highers, skateboarding ramps and half-pipes in people's backyards. Soon enough, his good friend Clint joined him. And not long after, Mark Deymaz (then the youth pastor for Central Bible Church in Portland) shelled out some money to build ramps in the church parking lot. He encouraged Paul and Clint to "let the kids skate, with a plan to 'preach Jesus' and then see what happens."

"PAUL ANDERSON MADE IT HIS MISSION TO HANG OUT WITH SKATERS AND IN HIS OWN WAY, BECOME A 'FISHER OF MEN.'"

Today, Paul continues to do just that, along with his current ministry partner, Ben Thomas. But now they actually hold church inside a skate park that's more than eleven thousand square feet in its entirety. Known to have the best runs in the Pacific Northwest, Paul, Ben, and forty staff members run SKATECHURCH each night. Kids come in to skate the bowl, quarter pipes, banks, euro-gaps, handrails, and two indoor street courses. And in the middle of every skate session, everyone lays down their board for a thirty-minute message. For those without a baseball hat or headband to stop the sweat, the back of their hand will suffice as they slide their lean frames into worn-out folding chairs, ears alert to a straight-forward presentation of the Gospel.

Tragically, Clint passed away over ten years after contracting HIV through a contaminated blood transfusion he'd received following a near fatal motorcycle accident. Ben commented, "Most of the kids know the history of SKATECHURCH, and we keep Clint's VW bus, photograph, and his board in the skate park as a memorial to his service to Christ and the skaters of Portland."

Paul Anderson, now in his forties, is known as somewhat of a legend—in contemporary ministry as well as in skateboarding history. "It really is incredible to think about how God was able to do all this over the past few decades. More than ten thousand young people have heard the Gospel through SKATECHURCH. More than one thousand of them made decisions to turn their lives over to Jesus. I think that is not only a testament to the power of the Gospel, but also to what can happen when you bring church to the people instead of trying to drag people into church."

Talk about a relevant way to worship—nothing is fragmented for these skaters. Their perspective on life is shaped by their passion: skateboarding. And now they are able to skate in a place that not only reflects what they value physically and mentally, but also spiritually. For a generation that has been labeled postmodern, where truth is so fragmented it no longer exists except within one's mind, and then only for a fleeting moment, here are representatives from that generation who have brought all the pieces back together and created a world that makes sense. With Stavesacre and Blindside blaring in the background, they're getting on their boards and worshiping God— not only with their minds, but also with their bodies.

"NOW THEY ACTUALLY HOLD CHURCH INSIDE AN ELEVEN THOUSAND SQUARE FOOT SKATE PARK. TALK ABOUT A RELEVANT WAY TO WORSHIP—NOTHING IS FRAGMENTED FOR THESE SKATERS."

Ben Thomas added, "The Apostle Paul encouraged the Corinthians, 'Whatever you do, whether you eat or drink, to do it all to the glory of God,' and as difficult as this commandment is to follow for the majority of Christians, I know now more and more young people are able to do just that. SKATECHURCH is just one example of how people can integrate their worship for God with their talent and passion."

What originally started as a nightly session of skate boarding and preaching quickly grew into an emerging extreme sport church movement. Now, skate churches exist worldwide, many modeled after Paul and Clint's original setup, everywhere from California to Canada. In addition, countless churches have built skate parks on church property or support local skate parks as part of their youth ministry.

"The best part is," Ben said, "kids come to SKATECHURCH who would never even think about walking into a traditional church."

Take Phil, for example. He was desperate to be somebody, like most teenagers, and consequently filled his life with whatever was popular: girls, sex, drugs, skateboarding. When he heard about SKATE-CHURCH, he came like all the rest—just to skate the best ramps in town. But, once inside the doors, he suddenly felt a deep sense of loneliness and futility sweep over him. He was also blown away by the integrity of the other skaters: They seemed secure in themselves and were satisfied to lay aside their worship of the board for the worship of God. They definitely had something he wanted.

Phil continued to come to SKATECHURCH, and not only just to skate the ramps. Rather, he was intrigued by the difference he saw in the lives of the skate staff and the love and acceptance they were showing him.

Through the Bible messages and one-on-one interaction with SKATECHURCH staff, Phil gave his life to Jesus. He is now attending a Bible college and even serves on the SKATECHURCH preaching staff. For Paul, Ben, and the others, being able to witness the transformation in Phil's life has been absolutely incredible.

It's guys like Phil that motivated Paul and Ben to expand the original purpose of SKATECHURCH. With the help of a strong staff of interns, Paul's priority has always been to "keep God first." From day one, he's ensured that a clear Gospel message is presented to those in attendance. Weekly accountability groups, Bible study, and discipleship programs have always been offered. But still, even with all this, they knew something was still lacking.

Having first encouraged the new followers of Christ to attend Sunday morning services at Central Bible, Paul began to realize that an alternative service would better meet the unique heart language these kids spoke. Since three out of four of the young people attending SKATECHURCH come from a broken home, and they really have their own dress code and lingo, it was difficult for them to fit into a traditional church service.

Already, there were a growing number of skateboarders who'd begun to share their testimonies, lead Bible studies, and meet with younger skaters just for the purpose of encouragement and friendship. Combined with the fact that some of them were talented musicians, they decided to start a worship and teaching Bible study, which quickly grew into an alternative-style Sunday evening church service for SKATECHURCH staff, skaters, and their friends and families at Central Bible.

"THIS IS WHAT CAN HAPPEN WHEN YOU BRING CHURCH TO THE PEOPLE INSTEAD OF TRYING TO DRAG PEOPLE INTO CHURCH."

House lights dim as band members open up the evening with songs that invite attendees to set aside some of their innate inhibitions for an extended time of joyful, exuberant worship. The welcoming, safe, and casual ambiance is met with appreciation. Without breaking a beat, the rhythm slows, and with hands held high and eyes shut, a more melodious tune ushers worshipers to the feet of Jesus for a time of communion. Remembering together what was accomplished for them at the cross, believers spend a moment in silent prayer. Gripped by the undeserved love and favor Jesus has poured out on them, they take the bread and the juice, which speak to them of the forgiveness offered through His body given and blood shed.

What follows can only be described as a simple, no-nonsense, honest-to-goodness, "tell-it-like-it-is" Bible message. And thankfully, some of those who are hurting, searching for answers, and hungry for significance, are placing their trust in Christ.

Paul and the SKATECHURCH staff know their listeners have a strong desire to belong. They want to be part of a community of people who understand them for who they are and will love and accept them. He also knows the hardness of life outside the doors of SKATECHURCH is a reality with which to be reckoned. Many of the feet who've crossed the threshold of SKATECHURCH haven't returned—not because of lack of desire. Tragically, it's because they've lost their lives through a heist gone south, one too many pills, a car accident, or illness. "Candy-coated messages," Paul said, "are certainly not what these kids are looking for when they come to church. They'd really rather have us tell it to them straight."

Combined with a rare form of boldness, compelling authority, and genuine compassion, Paul and the skate staff give them a cause other than skateboarding to live for—Jesus Christ.

**" LET US NOT GIVE UP MEETING TOGETH-
ER, AS SOME ARE IN THE HABIT OF DOING,
BUT LET US ENCOURAGE ONE ANOTHER—
AND ALL THE MORE AS YOU SEE THE DAY
APPROACHING. "**

—HEBREWS 10:25

05

DREAMING UP OUTRAGEOUS SCHEMES WITH GOD

BY IAN NICHOLSON

IT WAS A COLD JANUARY DAY AS JUSTIN,

a soft spoken prophetic type, meandered along the beach with Pete Greig—kicking the pebbles, chatting about trivia, and gently musing about life, when he said, "You know, Pete, I think I have only ever had one dream—to be part of a movement, alongside real friends, doing something significant for God."

The four days in Malaga, Spain, had been an intense time of praying, planning, and dreaming, as the annual 24-7 Round Table was drawing to a close. Each person was sharing their high point of the gathering, and Mexican leader Carlos Sanchez was unusually serious. "The absolute high point for me was Ian's talk on mission," he said. I tried to look humble, but smiled a little too smugly, and a few people noticed. Carlos continued, "As Ian was speaking, my mind wandered, and I looked over at the building opposite us, where a workman on the third floor pointed outwards and peed down onto the street below and then just went back to work. It was so funny—I'll remember that more than anything else." I laughed with everyone else and perhaps a little too loud.

"FOR 24-7, THERE WAS NO BIG IDEA, FIVE-YEAR PLAN, BUDGET, OR EVEN STRATEGY. IT WAS AN ACCIDENT AND HAS LEFT THOSE INVOLVED PERPETUALLY BEWILDERED."

That was in 1999, the 24-7 saga was just beginning, and, to be honest, was in danger of overwhelming us. Every day there were more surprises, opportunities, and requests. Every time we edged toward complacency, some new story of a healing or a miraculous prayer answered would leave us speechless—it was a blur. Alongside this, there was genuine heartbreaking struggle as we faced our own personal needs and issues. As Pete gently spoke to us, he began to cry, but carried on anyway: "You know, if God wants to say 'stop' or if it all goes wrong, I just hope one thing—that we stay friends and that ten years from now, we'll be drinking lots of espresso together and still dreaming up outrageous schemes with God.'"

THE PRAYER ROOMS

Praying 24-7 day in and day out did seem outrageous at the time. But since the first prayer room began, people have been doing just that: pleading with God every hour of the day, every day of the week. As you begin to read this chapter, there are groups of people praying, rooms full of them worldwide. Some rooms will be large-scale city affairs, while others will be a small room with a group of friends. It could be on any continent—near the equator, above the Arctic Circle, in a California suburb, or in an Indian slum. And every room has one thing in common: They are linked to an explosion of continuous prayer, 24-7.

Just imagine the prayers—whether a student in stillness and solitude at 4 a.m. or a business executive taking time away from the incessant emails and phone calls to touch base with God. There will be children, families, old ladies (of course, there are always old ladies praying!), and, perhaps most surprisingly, there will be young people—lots and lots of them. Some will be weeping their way into the Father's presence, others will be reading their Bibles—perhaps for the first time in weeks—and others will be painting a prophetic prayer on the wall.

The global movement that has become 24-7 prayer is a phenomenon that is capturing the lives and dreams of a whole generation. However, in the "How to Start A Movement for Christ" manuals, it's never laid out like this. For 24-7, there was no big idea, five-year plan, budget, or even strategy. It was an accident and has left those involved perpetually bewildered—and perhaps that's half the fun. In the beginning, all it took was a group of friends dreaming of doing something significant together for God. About five years ago, they took an empty room, let loose their creativity, and then started to pray nonstop—whispering their prayers, shouting and weeping their requests, dancing and painting. Hundreds of names of friends were written on the wall, and quite a few are now vibrant Christians. Phil, the 24-7 office manager, was, in September 1999, one of the scribbled names on a wall, and now he is central to the entire movement. It was electric—there were stories of angelic encounters, unexpected financial provisions, and miraculous healings, and young people's lives were being changed in the presence of God.

And then it spread—not as another over-marketed cool idea, but like a secret too good to keep to yourself—the idea spread from friend to friend and group to group. Since September 1999, more than twenty-two hundred prayer rooms in more than fifty nations have formed, all for nonstop prayer. There have been rooms in police stations, cafés, universities, breweries, army bases, and rock festivals. Instead of disengaging from a seemingly irrelevant church culture or settling into mediocrity and cynicism, tens of thousands of twentysomethings are being awakened to the fact that God is at work in their generation and in their world. And it's been amazing to read the stories of unexpected encounters with a living God:

"Jesus is so near in the prayer room. Sometimes all of us weep for the lost. People just want to pray—we don't have to encourage them ... we have received vision, passion, and a love for our nation and this generation." (Ocke, Germany)

"THE GLOBAL MOVEMENT THAT HAS BECOME 24-7 PRAYER IS A PHENOMENON THAT IS CAPTURING THE LIVES AND DREAMS OF A WHOLE GENERATION."

"For years I've been trying to get young people to have a heart for the lost and a desire to pray. Last night I found eight of them on their faces in the prayer room at 2 a.m. weeping for their non-Christian friends—what is happening?" (Youth leader, Spain)

"The week exceeded all our expectations—over two hundred people used the prayer room from twenty churches. People were saved, the lukewarm ignited, and unity made huge steps forward. Through 24-7, a radical vision was imparted way beyond anything our puny little talks can accomplish." (Pastor, U.K.)

And then there are the hundreds who have expressed simple sentiments like Sarah: "We left the room at 4:35 a.m. madly and passionately in love with Jesus."

THE VISION

What's the vision? What's the big idea?

The vision? The vision is JESUS—obsessively, dangerously, undeniably Jesus.

The vision is an army of young people. You see bones? I see an army.
And they are FREE from materialism ... they are mobile like the wind, they
belong to the nations.

The words above are extracted from what is now known as "The
Vision," a poem, prophecy, and prayer that was scrawled on the wall
of the first prayer room. When I first read it, it sent shivers down my
spine—to me it was a mandate for a movement and connects with
dreams and aspirations in a remarkable way. In the last five years, "The
Vision" has been filmed, choreographed, mixed by DJs, and repro-
duced in many nations. This visionary prayer unveils that 24-7 is more
than just a side-blinded prayer movement. It is outward; it "belongs to
nations." It does not just bless believers, but goes beyond the isolated
ghetto of Christian culture. God spoke clearly that He was already at
work way beyond our meetings. He spoke clearly that He wanted us
to join Him at some of His meetings. And these can be in the most
surprising places!

The beautiful, mystical island of Ibiza in the Mediterranean has been
referred to as the "Sodom and Gomorrah" of Europe by the U.K.
tabloid press. The club scene of Ibiza attracts tens of thousands each
summer to drunken, drugged up weeks of excess in some of the biggest clubs in the world. When, at the invitation of the local churches,
we took our first team to pray and reach out in the bars of Ibiza, we
didn't quite know what to expect. It was definitely a step into the
unknown. Again, the impact on us was remarkable—we watched
people come alive in a way they never would have at home. One girl,
Bex, simply said, "This is what I was made for!" Josie commented that
she had experienced more of the power of God in the Holy Spirit's
meetings in the pubs, clubs, and streets than she ever had in a church
meeting. Jez, who made a television documentary about the mission,
said, "People all over town are talking about 24-7. I keep overhear-
ing discussions about the work it is doing—it's made a tremendous
impact."

There were some startling healings during that time, but perhaps the biggest impact from the first year had to do with the weather. Ibiza had had a total drought for three-and-a-half years and no rain in July for twenty-five years. A major focus of prayer was for the drought to break, and one Sunday evening after an open air worship service with the island's churches, the first drops of rain began to fall, leading to the entire island being lashed by rainstorms for twenty-four hours. This eventually brought considerable media attention, but more importantly, it pointed to the heavens opening over Ibiza and a change in the spiritual climate.

The conviction is that we have to move out of our safety zones to connect with the full purposes of God. It's not about mission teams, but about mission as life. We are taking 24-7 prayer and sacrificial outreach to the high places of youth culture—the music festivals, clubbing areas, party zones, and surf beaches—in places like the Balkans, Brazil, Mexico, Spain, and Cyprus. These are places where God already is and wants us to be in His name.

THE BOILER ROOMS

As well as prayer and mission, the third strand of this young movement is the boiler rooms—intentional 24-7 communities focused on prayer, devotion to Christ, creativity, mission, and service to the poor at the heart of towns and cities. In many ways, they have been likened to the monasteries, which were so effective in turning the tide of paganism across Europe. They are giving people a hands-on way of living out the 24-7 values—marrying intimacy with God with sacrificial involvement with the world.

Again, they have taken everyone by surprise! When a derelict drinking house in Reading, U.K., was turned into the first boiler room, it was expected that prayer would be the main activity. Instead the house became a magnet for local young people—many who walked in drunk, drugged, or were heavily into the occult. It became a more popular skate venue than the official town skate park, and during the months, many opened up to believers there and to God in a way they never would have before.

"HOW DO YOU GO ABOUT CHANGING THE WORLD? JESUS SIMPLY GATHERED A GROUP OF FRIENDS, SHARED HIS LOVE FOR THE FATHER, AND THEN SAID, 'GO AND MAKE A DIFFERENCE IN MY NAME.'"

Andy Freeman (also known as "The Abbott") commented that he spent seventeen years being a church youth worker wanting to reach those with real needs and being largely frustrated. He then had a more effective youth ministry in seventeen months running a prayer house! It was not all easy though, and after a particularly harrowing weekend when a young drug addict friend was buried, Andy wrote, "I've got nothing left to give except me. Maybe in our weakness and pain is where God's voice is at its loudest. Maybe the place we've spent years trying to run away from is the very place to be."

"In the last days, God says, I will pour out my Spirit on all people. Your sons and daughters will prophesy, your young men will see visions, your old men will dream dreams ... The sun will be turned to darkness and the moon to blood before the coming of the great and glorious day of the Lord" (Joel 2).

So what is happening? Has 24-7 simply "struck it lucky," or is there a more profound reason why God is drawing hundreds of thousands to pray like they never have before? As a twenty-one-year-old backpacker, Pete Greig (who was the catalyst behind the first prayer room) had an open-eyed vision one night. He recalls, "My eyes were open, but I could 'see' with absolute clarity before me the different countries laid out like an atlas. From each one a faceless army of young people rose from the page, crowds of them in every nation awaiting orders."

THE ARMY

Could this be the core issue? Is God raising up an army, and if so, where are the conscripts? Are the whispers of God in the prayer rooms calling and shaping a generation across the nations? Are the healings, miracles, conversions, and answers to prayer pointing to a much larger scale movement of God? Often a 24-7 week is launched with a corporate "war cry" as hundreds yell out "Come On!" in a powerful *Braveheart* style as a call to God and encouragement to each other. The first time I took part in a war cry, I knew something was being unleashed—a Jesus movement of nobodies with prayer, mission, and community at the core.

As a pastor whose dream for many years has been to see a fresh mission movement among the young, 24-7 connects supernaturally with the instincts of the emerging culture. It loves and affirms the traditional Church but also releases a fresh breath from heaven and shows us the true Church is the body of Christ, and right now, worldwide, the body is praying, and it won't stop. 24-7 has inspired this generation to "take hold of that for which Jesus has taken hold of them." It calls out to the back pews and gives permission to initiate, be creative, and "let the dreams out." Time and again we meet people—whether in Berlin, Barcelona, Calgary, Mexico, or California—who "are connected" to 24-7 and know it's what they want to give their lives to. It has captured them.

"THE FIRST TIME I TOOK PART IN A WAR CRY, I KNEW THAT SOMETHING WAS BEING UNLEASHED—A JESUS MOVEMENT OF NOBODIES WITH PRAYER, MISSION, AND COMMUNITY AT THE CORE."

How do you go about changing the world? Jesus simply gathered a group of friends, shared His love for the Father, gave them a few radical dreams, and then said, "Go and make a difference in my name."

Who can join 24-7? Well, it's a movement, so anyone can and nobody can. 24-7 is an invitation from heaven to find friends, seek God, drink coffee, and dream together of what you can do—that's the Jesus way to change the world. Imagine the prayer rooms again—imagine the prayers. Can you see yourself there? Are you ready for the call of the Father?

Don't hold back.

> **EVERY BELIEVER NEEDS A 'CHURCH'— EVEN IF IT'S JUST FOUR OR FIVE OF YOU MEETING TOGETHER TO WORSHIP. I KNOW MY RELATIONSHIP WITH CHRIST WOULD DETERIORATE IF I DIDN'T SURROUND MYSELF WITH PEOPLE WHO ENCOURAGE AND CHALLENGE ME IN MY FAITH.**
>
> **—PHILIP EVANS**
> SURREY, ENGLAND, AGE TWENTY-THREE

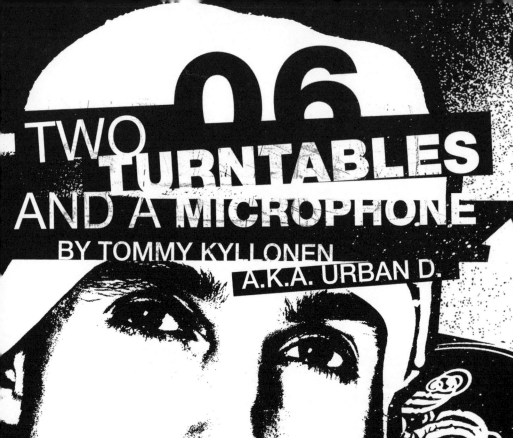

06

TWO TURNTABLES
AND A MICROPHONE

BY TOMMY KYLLONEN
A.K.A. URBAN D.

CROSSOVER COMMUNITY CHURCH STARTED WITH A community of people who wanted something different, something real. They were burned out on organized religion—tired of the politics, the tradition, the masks people hid behind at traditional churches. They saw the needs of the people on the street that weren't being met, and they wanted to do something about it. That's when Pastor Joe McCuthen and Al Palmquist sought my wife and I out and presented us with a challenge: to create an urban youth ministry from the ground up.

I grew up in church as a pastor's kid, and honestly, I saw some pretty ugly things behind the scenes. My parents were always on point, but many times, the church board, and some of the other leaders, had their own agenda. They didn't like change, and their agendas usually had nothing to do with God. As a young kid, this was pretty confusing. Growing up as a teenager in Philadelphia, the street life quickly attracted me. Hip-hop became my world, as I was engulfed in rap music, graffiti tagging, break dancing, and playing b-ball. I made my share of mistakes as I began hanging with the wrong crowd. My family continued to pray for me and tried to guide me in the right direction. Eventually, I recommitted my life to Christ my senior year in high school and began to seek His direction for my future, but even that was a journey rather than a straight path.

After graduation from high school, I attended a Christian college, but once again, I headed in the other direction and got involved in clubbing, partying, and chillin' with friends who did not have a real relationship with God. Conviction began to set in during my second semester, as I realized I was such a fake. What was I doing at a Christian college anyway? It was a turning point. Shortly after that, I got involved in a homeless ministry in the subways of Philly and started working with an urban youth ministry in the city, and God used these things to break me.

"HIP-HOP BECAME MY WORLD, AS I WAS ENGULFED IN RAP MUSIC, GRAFFITI TAGGING, BREAK DANCING, AND PLAYING B-BALL."

My heart was broken, and my eyes were opened. I looked around and began to see all the needs in the very streets I chilled in. My calling from my Creator became clear. I knew I was called to reach this culture and translate His message of hope to my people. This led me to transfer my sophomore year to a college in Florida, where I really began to focus on my relationship with Christ and my education. It was also during this time that I met my future wife, Lucy LaGuerra, who was from New York City and also had similar goals. We both were so sure that we would be led back up North to be part of a ministry in a major city like Philly, but God had different plans. In 1996, he led us to Crossover in Tampa, Florida.

My desire was to start something fresh and new that would be relevant to urban unchurched kids. I wasn't aware of any current ministry models, but I knew I didn't want to do church the way it had always been done. I knew, and the pastor knew, that wouldn't work here—so he gave me full freedom to do whatever I felt necessary. Lucy and I didn't receive a regular salary or any benefits, but we learned to trust God to provide. I began to record my first hip-hop album with Christ-centered lyrics and stories of what I've been through. Between my music, my wife's job, and some outside supporters, we got by. We started basketball leagues, did hip-hop concerts, and started a youth service on a separate night. Since I grew up in the same environment, just in a different city, I connected at a deep level with these kids. By the end of the first year, we had close to sixty youth attending, and we actually outnumbered the adult congregation.

March 14, 1998, was the date of our first official Fla.vor Alliance hip-hop concert at the church. We made flyers and got the word out in the streets, at schools, and at other church youth groups. Carlos Ramirez (a.k.a. Los 1) was a Fla.vor member who invited his boy E.J. (a.k.a. Spec) from college. He had been talking to him about God and had been trying to get him to come out to one of the events for a while. That night, Spec showed up, and his stereotypes of "church" were completely shattered, as he walked into the concert and saw more than three hundred other people who looked just like him. He never expected to see a real hip-hop concert at a church! Spec was eighteen-years-old and grew up in a rough single parent home, moving back and forth between Tampa and New York. He grew up Catholic and was even an altar boy as a child, but wanted nothing to do with church or God at this point in his life. Hip-hop was his god. But that night, his Creator spoke to him loud and clear and in a language he understood. And he responded to the invitation at the end of the service to receive Christ. I called Spec the next week and invited him to come out to the Thursday night youth service. He came and became a regular part of our community.

As Spec grew in his relationship with Christ, he began to tell others. He invited his coworker Melissa, who was into hip-hop, but was also skeptical since her family never went to church. Melissa knew something was missing in her life, and she had a lot of questions about God. But as she continued to come to Crossover, God began to break down all the walls of mistrust in her heart. She soon built a relationship with Christ and began getting more and more involved. It's been amazing to watch her grow. Six years later, she is now one of the key leaders at our ministry, as she leads the choir and is involved in worship and our Turnstyle junior high service.

In college, Spec studied graphic art and design, and one of his passions was graffiti art. Before he gave his life to Christ, he used his talent to portray an angry, negative message in the streets. But now, Spec works full time as the media department director at our church. He uses his creativity and talent to design our website, video productions, and print material all to God's glory.

In 1998, the founding pastor of Crossover left to be an evangelist, and over the next three and a half years, the church had two different pastors who both had full-time jobs outside the church. Because of their need to work and their lack of time, the church struggled to grow and remained at about forty members. However, the youth ministry had grown to close to two hundred attending, and most of the adult members were now part of the church as a result of their involvement in the youth ministry.

When the last pastor decided to leave, he and the church council asked me to step up and take the position of the pastor. I was scared. I was reluctant. I was overwhelmed. Here I was, a husband, a youth pastor with hundreds of kids, and a national hip-hop artist who traveled frequently and averaged about seven concerts a month. How could I handle any more responsibilities? My wife and I took inventory and realized it wasn't about us or what we wanted. Many of our members already looked to me as the pastor because I was at the church on a full-time basis, ran the day-to-day operations, and took care of some of the responsibilities the other pastors were unable to. We had sacrificed and invested six years of our lives to see this incredibly unique, first of its kind, hip-hop flavored youth ministry develop and touch so many lives. We loved our teens, our young adults, and our leaders. And now the church needed a pastor. We knew God was calling us to step up.

"I WASN'T AWARE OF ANY CURRENT MINISTRY MODELS, BUT I KNEW I DIDN'T WANT TO DO CHURCH THE WAY IT HAD ALWAYS BEEN DONE."

In the beginning of 2002, I took the position as senior pastor, which was a smooth transition for just about everyone but me. Jim Dell, a friend and leader at the ministry, pushed me during this time. He helped me with preaching, planning, and learning how to be the kingpin. I also got mentored by other pastors, read several books, and most of all sought God. The church never really had a clear direction, as it changed pastors several times since I had been there. God quickly made it clear that our purpose was to reach the hip-hop culture. We were already known in many circles as "the hip-hop church" since we used so many elements of the culture in our youth services.

But, could this work as the whole vision of a church? It had never been done before. Our leadership team went on a weekend retreat, came up with a mission statement, and began to brainstorm how our church could become more effective. We left knowing our mission is "to relevantly introduce the truth of Christ to the hip-hop culture, as we develop worship, purpose, unity, and leadership in their lives."

Crossover began to change the way we did "church" on Sundays. Everything we did, from our prayers to the worship and the messages, had to be relevant and understandable for everyone who walked through our doors. We incorporated a DJ on turntables playing hip-hop/R&B instrumentals during worship with rappers mixed in. We installed soft recess lighting in the main auditorium, along with a hazer and colored gel lights to illuminate the stage area. TV screens hang from the ceiling and display images, PowerPoint, and even music videos and movie clips to illustrate messages. All these things set the atmosphere for people to come in and feel comfortable. Services became exciting. People really began to connect with their Creator. The word began to spread, and many new people began to visit.

A few years ago, Adam (a.k.a. Lucky) sat in his room contemplating suicide. He had been addicted to alcohol and cocaine for several years. Lucky heard about Crossover from his family, and as he sat in his room, he kept hearing this voice inside telling him to call me at Crossover. But Adam and I had never even met. Soon enough, his mom called me, and later he sat in my office and poured out his heart about his life and his unhappiness. By the end of the conversation, we prayed, and he invited Christ to be the Leader of his life. His life has taken a total one-eighty turn. Lucky has had the opportunity to share his story with thousands these past few years. Today he is a committed Christian who is an active part of our church family.

"NOW OUR MISSION IS TO RELEVANTLY INTRODUCE THE TRUTH OF CHRIST TO THE HIP-HOP CULTURE, AS WE DEVELOP PURPOSE, WORSHIP, UNITY, AND LEADERSHIP IN THEIR LIVES."

As the church continued to grow, we built a large patio area outside with seating to create a place to build community. It has become a place where people hang out, eat, talk, and build relationships before and after services. Our lobby is the home of our Hip-Hop Shop, where we carry more than ninety Christian hip-hop and R&B CDs, along with DVDs, vinyl, magazines, and drinks. Graffiti murals cover several walls on the outside and inside of our building. A twelve-foot by twelve-foot wooden dance floor is built in the back of our main auditorium for our break dancers. Talent Develop classes for breaking, rapping, DJing, acting, singing, and more have become a great discipleship tool that is connected with our small group Bible studies on Tuesday nights. Our Thursday night youth service has been split into two separate services by age groups in order to fit everyone and better meet their needs.

Crossover recently put in a full basketball court and a seven thousand square foot skate park. As we continue to better meet the needs of our community, we continue to see incredible growth. We also recently started a second Sunday morning service to accommodate the three hundred-plus people who now attend. With all the lives that have been changed and miracles that have taken place at our grassroots ministry, we know this is just the beginning. Many ministries have looked to our church and our youth ministry as a model the past few years. As a result, every November, we hold our annual Hip-Hop/ Urban Ministries Conference at Crossover called Fla.vor Fest. Since 1996, I've recorded five solo albums and also had the opportunity to travel to Germany, Japan, England, and across the U.S. performing and speaking at conferences.

Our staff and leaders have stayed committed as we stepped out of the box to reach this culture. They believe in the vision since they are all actively a part of it and have watched it unfold. As a result, God has built a growing multicultural family of young urban adults who are passionately worshiping Him!

❝ I LOVE THE DIVERSITY OF CHURCH—SO MANY DIFFERENT PEOPLE SAVED FROM A RANGE OF PAIN, ADDICTIONS, LIFESTYLES—NOW ALL SET FREE IN A COMMUNITY TOGETHER. ❞

—JAMES BULLOCK
LIVERPOOL, ENGLAND, AGE TWENTY-FOUR

07

COME TO THE TO THE BRIDEGROOM

BY MIKE BICKLE

MY STORY IS ONE OF A SPIRITUALLY BORED BELIEVER
who was ignited by the revelation of Jesus as a Bridegroom God, a God with fiery affection for me. When I say Bridegroom God, I am talking about a God who is tender in His dealings with your weaknesses. He is glad, He is fiery in His affections for you, and He has transcendent beauty—a beauty from another realm.

But this is not the God who's talked about at church. So if you haven't experienced a deep encounter with the Holy Spirit, and you've been going to church for as long as you remember, or maybe you walked out of church because it didn't seem like a place where you could really find God, that is about to change.

We are at a critical point in history. Right now, the Holy Spirit is wooing His Church. He wants it to be fully in sync with His vision and intentions. As God woos His Church, He is transforming it. He is making us a passionate, transcendent, power-filled body of believers. I can say this because I see things changing—rapidly, every day. God is awakening the human heart and calling us to be fascinated and exhilarated with Him. We were created by a passionate God, and He wants us to live full-throttle.

Millions of people your age in Asia, Africa, Europe, South America, and North America are saying, "Lord, I want to be on of these radical, lovesick worshipers of Jesus."

It is one thing to want to be extreme or radical, but it is an entirely different thing to put that together with the heart of a lovesick worshiper. I know this from experience. The gap between wanting to be radical and actually being equipped to walk it out is answered in the revelation of Jesus as a Bridegroom God. You will burn out from being extreme if you don't have anything to fuel it. Encounters with God are what fuel passion. They make us radical worshipers of Jesus.

"I SO WANTED TO BE RADICAL FOR JESUS IN MY YOUTH, BUT I REALLY DID HATE PRAYER."

We crave the encounter we get when we experience Jesus as the passionate Bridegroom God who feels so deeply toward us. At International House of Prayer (I.H.O.P.) in Kansas City, we identify ourselves as the Church with a bridal identity. It is the Church with a bridal intimacy that cries, "Come, Lord Jesus."

And we cannot have personal encounters with God, true intimacy with our Bridegroom, without prayer. A lifestyle of prayer is the key to a life of radical encounters with God. I so wanted to be radical for Jesus in my youth, but I really did hate prayer. Who could have imagined that one day I would be leading a 24/7 worship and prayer ministry?

"WE ARE AT A CRITICAL POINT IN HISTORY. RIGHT NOW, THE HOLY SPIRIT IS WOOING HIS CHURCH. HE WANTS IT TO BE FULLY IN SYNC WITH HIS VISION AND INTENTIONS."

Just as I was once a spiritually bored believer who was set on fire by the revelation of Jesus as a Bridegroom God, I am not alone. God has graciously helped a growing company of weak and broken believers in Kansas City to give themselves to nonstop worship and intercession since September 1999—yes, twenty-four hours a day for over four years. The core of our twenty-four-hour prayer ministry is a mandate to raise up a young adult prayer, worship, and prophetic movement.

Currently, we have about four hundred full-time staff, with another three hundred students and/or interns. In other words, we have more than seven hundred mostly young adults in our ministry here who are pursuing a lifestyle of fasting, worship, prayer, and outreach. Staff members raise their own support and are courageous missionaries doing the work of intercession that is so necessary in this generation. They are weak missionaries, but courageous ones—courageous enough to believe in the love of God that is stronger than our weakness.

The transformation of my life from bored to exhilarated began with a supernatural encounter with the Lord in July 1988. From that day on, I saw Jesus as more than a King who possesses all the power of God. I launched out in a journey of seeing God very differently than what religious tradition teaches. And to see Jesus as the beautiful God who has a heart of burning desire for me changed the way I approach prayer, fasting, and holiness.

Many of the young people in our ministry have experienced a similar transformation. They have come here because their church or college ministry is not taking them deep into God's Spirit. They were not encountering God or experiencing intimacy with their Bridegroom Jesus. They came because of the longing in their hearts to radically encounter their God.

We train them in the precepts of how to operate in the Holy Spirit, how to understand bridal intimacy, how to understand the generation in which we live and the hour the Lord returns. They have a chance here to learn and then use that knowledge in practical ways through outreach and ministry.

One of our interns told me he loves going downtown and ministering to the poor of Kansas City. He said he has actually come to understand who Jesus is in a greater way by being who Jesus is to the people on the street. This is fantastic.

The mission base is our focal point. We have eight ministries, with the House of Prayer as the centerpiece—the prayer furnace of the mission base. We have healing rooms where we regularly pray for the sick, prophetic teams that prophesy to hundreds of people every week, and all kinds of ministry outreaches in the area.

"THE CORE OF OUR TWENTY-FOUR-HOUR PRAYER MINISTRY IS A MANDATE TO RAISE UP A YOUNG ADULT PRAYER, WORSHIP, AND PROPHETIC MOVEMENT."

All of our ministries are based in Kansas City, so the synergism creates an environment of like-minded people where we can get the most intense experience of being saturated in our values. Whether people are interceding or worshiping in the prayer rooms, ministering in the healing or prophetic rooms, taking a Bible class or working with the poor, they are encountering God and going deep in Him.

A lot of the time I get asked how we get young adults to be disciplined. How do we get them to pray for hours at a time? I say, "Give them a vision. You will never disciple them until their hearts are connected to a vision that has their name on it. That is how you disciple a young person. Connect their heart to a vision they believe in."

We have all ages in this ministry. It is fantastic to see nine-year-olds interceding, laying hands on the sick, and prophesying. They are committed because God has touched their hearts. We have teenaged worship leaders, musicians, and singers. They come to the prayer room because they long to touch God. They are going after God because He is all they want and what they hunger for.

We are disciplined by desire being awakened in the innermost parts of our hearts. Awakened desire has caused me to do more things in the line of obedience than any fear of getting into trouble or any other motivation. Not because I have to—I want to! It is my destiny. Awakened desire is the answer for the young adult movement in the earth.

I have heard many stories from the young adults here about how they were living a life without purpose before they walked through our doors. "I didn't know who I was or what I was called to do," one intern told me. Her parents made her come here. She had no direction for her life, was confused, and practically got out of the car screaming as her parents dropped her off. But as she was exposed to the Bridegroom God, her heart was melted in a matter of months.

Many come here out of bad situations. Some come straight out of jail, others off the streets. They have a similar cry: "I hit a wall; I hit bottom. I woke up saying enough is enough." They need drastic healing. And then they encounter God in the deep places of God's heart. For the first time, they are introduced to the gladness of God, the Bridegroom God who has a burning desire to be with them.

This is the greatest hour in history to be radical. This is the greatest hour in history to be a risk taker. Love is the key, and the Church needs to be radical lovers. To be radical lovers, the Church needs to be in full sync with the Holy Spirit. And one of the most significant things the Holy Spirit is doing right now is revealing Jesus as the Bridegroom God. Right now, God is revealing the identity of the Church as a cherished Bride—the cherished prize of God's heart.

When these realities fill the prayer movement, it will be different. When these realities fill the prophetic movement, it will be different. When these realities fill the preaching in mission movement, it will be different. Everything will change when we discover and encounter a Bridegroom God and the corresponding revelation—I am a cherished Bride.

"RIGHT NOW, GOD IS REVEALING THE IDENTITY OF THE CHURCH AS A CHERISHED BRIDE—THE CHERISHED PRIZE OF GOD'S HEART."

That is who we are. That is who you are. That is the truth that this generation is longing to hear. When we feel the bridal identity and touch that, we will say "come" in an entirely different way when we pray and worship. When our hearts are lovesick for God, we will also be effective in calling others to God. The cry "come" is not just vertically to Jesus. The cry "come" becomes horizontal. We are calling the nations to Him as well—and not just to God; we are calling the nations to a Bridegroom God. That is a different message.

"WHEN I HEAR THE WORD 'CHURCH,' I THINK OF THE BODY OF CHRIST IN ITS FULLNESS, WITHOUT DENOMINATIONAL OR DOGMATIC BOUNDARIES, CHURCH IN ALL ITS ORGANIC GLORY, SHIFTING AND GROWING, AS ALL LIVING THINGS DO."

—ANDY SQUYRES
MOORESVILLE, NORTH CAROLINA,
AGE THIRTY

08

LOVE IS OF THE ESSENCE

BY TIMOTHY KEEL

I HAVE A CONFESSION TO MAKE: I LOVE THE CHURCH. I REALLY DO.

Maybe that doesn't seem like much of a confession to you, but in some circles, it is en vogue to express disdain, not love, for the Church—even among people who love God and long to make an impact in the world. To be fair, I also have to confess that I am often tempted in this direction as well. I can easily slip over into frustration and anger—even despair at times. You probably understand where I am coming from: When you love a person, his or her shortcomings can be the hardest to handle. People let us down, and that is hard to take. I am often afraid that the failures of others will reflect badly on me. I am invested. Organizations, full of people, let us down in the same kinds of ways. The Church is just such an organization.

Certainly there has been enough bad press in the life of the Church in the past two decades to make any of us wonder why we ought to bother. It is not surprising that I am often disappointed and frustrated. This is especially magnified when I look at the accelerated amount of change that is happening around me in our world, much of it exciting, some of it troubling. Turning to see how churches are responding, I am often confronted by organizations that spend significant resources focused on internal debates over insignificant issues, rather than communities seeking to discover ways of living and thinking theologically and missiologically in the ever expanding and shifting cultural landscape. But what can I do about it?

Unfortunately, many people are choosing to disengage.

And so at the outset of this discussion about whether or not the Church is relevant (and if so, what makes it that way), I have to say this: I love the Church. I love her. I write from the inside, from a position of commitment and covenant. I hope you read from the inside too. If not, I hope myself and others can persuade you to step inside, because I believe that anyone wanting to manifest the kingdom of God proclaimed by Jesus must deal with and through the Church, specifically the local church. Because you are reading this, I'll assume you want to engage. I have chosen to engage. Thus engaged, I am experiencing a life in God with the Church that I always hoped would be true. As I travel and speak and listen and learn, I am discovering others spread out around North America and the world experiencing the same thing. In these places, amid a great deal of diversity and adversity, I perceive the expansion of the kingdom of God into the surrounding culture.

For me, trying to describe what makes the Church relevant in one essay is near maddening. So I am going to focus on one thing I know. In
very broad terms, relevance begins and ends with love. The only way
I can experience love is among people. Most of the other things I believe are significant in terms of the relevance of the Church, especially
things related to creativity (which I believe is critical in our current
cultural environment), flow one way or another out of love and the
kinds of environments created where love is the primary currency.

"IN VERY BROAD TERMS, RELEVANCE BEGINS AND ENDS WITH LOVE. THE ONLY WAY I CAN EXPERIENCE LOVE IS AMONG PEOPLE."

So I say I love the Church, but that is not specific enough. I love the
local church. But even writing that isn't specific enough. See—I love
Matt, Don, Deanne, Lori, Todd, Mike, Shayne, Julie, Ruthie, Jerry, An-
sie, Mimi, Ora, Jason, Rebecca, Sacheen, Bill, Anna, Sam—really, more
people than I can name. I belong to these people, and they belong
to me. Together we belong to Jesus. It doesn't stop there: Because we
belong to Jesus, we belong to other communities of people who belong to Jesus. What's more, because of the love Jesus expresses for the
world, we belong to the world, too. Love creates belonging. Belonging
creates community. Belonging to Jesus creates communities of love.
Communities of love embody and expand the kingdom of God.

Jesus claimed this much: "A new command I give you: Love one
another. As I have loved you, so you must love one another. By this all
men will know that you are my disciples, if you love one another." We
embody our faith in meaningful ways when we are covenanted in love
to one another.

Duke theologian Stanley Hauerwas has influenced my ecclesiology (that is, my theology of the Church) greatly. Quoting one of the
principles of his mentor, the Mennonite theologian John Howard

Yoder, Hauerwas said: "The work of Jesus was not a new set of ideals or principles for reforming or even revolutionizing society, but the establishment of a new community, a people that embodied forgiveness, sharing and self-sacrificing love in its rituals and discipline. In that sense, the visible church is not to be the bearer of Christ's message; but to be the message."

"TOGETHER WE BELONG TO JESUS. IT DOESN'T STOP THERE: BECAUSE WE BELONG TO JESUS, WE BELONG TO OTHER COMMUNITIES OF PEOPLE WHO BELONG TO JESUS."

Now we know that the reality is that we must both bear and be the message. But I believe that we have the proclamation aspect down quite well. Too well. That the kingdom is meant to be embodied, that we are to be the message—that is what we must be reminded of with great regularity. I would even go so far to say that the message of Christ would go out more effectively if we would be willing to keep our mouths shut for a while and learn how to love.

Another one of my favorite authors says something similar. Recently passed away, Lesslie Newbigin spent thirty-five years of his life as a missionary in India. When he retired at sixty-five, he and his wife returned to England (by bus!) only to discover that Western civilization had domesticated Jesus and was in need of being engaged. His solution? Local communities of believers. He wrote: "How can this strange story of God made man, of a crucified savior, of resurrection and new creation become credible for those whose entire mental training has conditioned them to believe that the real world is the world that can be satisfactorily explained and managed without the hypothesis of God? I know of only one clue to the answering of that question, only one real hermeneutic of the gospel: congregations that believe it."

The Church belongs to Jesus. We are His people. Inasmuch as we are His disciples, living in the Jesus way, the Jesus truth, and the Jesus life, we participate in the divine life, the kingdom. This is always relevant because it flows out of the Creator and Redeemer of life itself. The life of the Church, then, is the Gospel! Or at least that is how I believe God intends it to be. This is what the historical Church meant when it stated that outside the Church, there is no salvation. Does that seem extreme to you? I hope not.

So a community of disciples is a collection of people living together meaningfully in the way of Jesus before God, each other, themselves, and the surrounding culture (of which they are also a part). Because I am a follower of Jesus, that means I am learning that loving people is costly, especially when our relationships are real. I am also learning to accept the fact that most of my life goes by in rather unremarkable ways; in fact, there is nothing very remarkable about our life together as a community called the local church. I'm pretty convinced that if you took some time to hang out around us, you'd be spectacularly unimpressed. We do things that millions of other people do every day, whether or not they belong to Jesus. Our lives are filled with laughter, boredom, frustration, tears, hugs, dishes, moments of inspiration, and instances of despair. I love and am loved. I have betrayed and been be-trayed. I forgive and am forgiven. As I share my life with these people, I have no guarantees of what will come from our shared life. In some seasons of my life, I am more available, and in other seasons, I am less. Sometimes when I am available, others are not. The life we are trying to live together is a complicated dance, but we are dancing. And we are doing all these things as disciples of Jesus Christ. This is spiritual formation. We are being transformed in the process. And people are watching.

And while in many ways our lives are normal and mundane and filled with the raw materials of simply being human, occasionally I experi-ence moments of absolute transcendence and awe. In times when I am often not paying attention, I get a glimpse of the glory of God through His people and have an inkling of why Jesus lived and died so that this bizarre entity called the Church could be constituted around His presence. I read what is written at the end of the first chapter of Ephesians, and I know it is true.

"All this energy issues from Christ: God raised him from death and set him on a throne in deep heaven, in charge of running the universe, everything from galaxies to governments, no name and no power exempt from his rule. And not just for the time being, but forever. He is in charge of it all, has the final word on everything. At the center of all this, Christ rules the church. The church, you see, is not peripheral to the world; the world is peripheral to the church. The church is Christ's body, in which he speaks and acts, by which he fills everything with his presence" (The Message).

Why do I take the time to write these things?

The "so what" for me lies in our individual and collective understanding of what the Church is and how it functions in the broader culture of which it is a part. For me, the Church is people. It is that simple. That is also why we are so easily disappointed and able to disappoint others.

That said, I acknowledge that a great deal of healthy questioning is going on around this topic today. As I said earlier, a great deal of cynicism, hand wringing, and posturing is going on also. Hopefully my contribution is in the former rather than the latter category, constructive rather than destructive. While there is no shortage of words and conversations in which to engage, ultimately how we live is our strongest statement of what we believe. That conviction is central to why I began a new church over five years ago. I wanted a living conversation with the Holy Spirit and other followers about what it means to be a disciple of Jesus today. This mission also began with the conviction (born out of experience) that the primary focus of faith is the local community of believers, however they are constituted.

Nearly everyone who thinks about such things recognizes that something significant is going on both inside and outside the culture of the Church. Almost everyone recognizes that broader cultural issues come to bear on this topic (like the impact of modernity and postmodernity, or whether or not we still live within Christendom, for example), though no one agrees exactly on what these issues are or how much weight they ought to carry. What makes the Church relevant? This line of questioning is a worthy one—one that has to be addressed as the institutional Church seems to be moving more and more to the margins of society (which I believe is extremely good news from a missiological perspective, because it changes our posture). However, I think this issue of relevance can be a slippery slope, so I also want some freedom to negotiate the terms of my "relevance."

"WHAT MAKES THE CHURCH RELEVANT? THIS LINE OF QUESTIONING IS A WORTHY ONE—ONE THAT HAS TO BE ADDRESSED AS THE INSTITUTIONAL CHURCH SEEMS TO BE MOVING MORE AND MORE TO THE MARGINS OF SOCIETY."

This is important, because there is an assumption that has infected the Church for as long as I can remember. The assumption is that there is something "out there" that is magical and mysterious and powerful. We think and dream and explore along these lines: "If only we can (re)discover _____X_____ (fill-in-the-blank: prayer, fasting, worship, community, drama, service) and implement it, then the Church will have _____Y_____ (fill-in-the-blank: impact, relevance, meaning, validity, profile, etc.)." We then scan the horizon looking for those places that have experienced a modicum of "success" and hope that whatever lightning they have captured will be bottled long enough to zap us as well. This is much easier, in the short-term, than living out the life of the Gospel in community.

As North American Christians, we must be wary. We have been well-discipled in the American notion of "technique." A technique is a "systematic procedure by which a complex or scientific task is accomplished." Techniques sound very promising. Reducing complex realities to methodology is dangerous, however. Fostered by a publishing culture looking for the next big thing to market, leaders jump from program to program in a desperate attempt to be relevant and make an impact, the whole while stifling their ability to discern and respond to the gentle voice of the Holy Spirit speaking to them from their heart, their community, their context, and the Scriptures. It is a truism that it is easier to adopt another person's or community's method (especially when it has been shown to increase the holy grail of American measurements: attendance and budget) than to sit patiently in your own closet, waiting desperately to hear the still small voice of God.

"FOR ME, THE CHURCH IS PEOPLE. IT IS THAT SIMPLE. THAT IS ALSO WHY WE ARE SO EASILY DISAPPOINTED AND ABLE TO DISAPPOINT OTHERS."

Let me say that I do believe that in the context where these packaged methods or techniques first were birthed, they came as an obedient move in response to the leading of God in concert with a community of people in a specific place. It is also true that there is great benefit to submitting ourselves to others who can lead us by their experience and knowledge. However, this is a very tricky move to execute in our culture: My experience has taught me that technique duplication is a very expedient short-term solution to the challenging issues we face as leaders. The long-term impact of technique-addiction has an increasingly short creative and spiritual attention span. Discipleship and shortcuts should not be comfortable bedmates. In leaders, they are deadly companions.

It seems to me that our churches have become quite efficient at sub-contracting our mission to specialists. The fifty-year-old practice of farming out engagement with the culture to various parachurch ministries (an effective and meaningful phenomenon that is understandable from a historical, theological, and missiological perspective) and program-centered projects will only ever be an addition or correction to something the larger body is lacking. But in my mind, it is always a last resort.

So that's a long way of saying that I'm not really sure what makes a church relevant, at least in any kind of way that could be described succinctly by me. But even if I could, I would be tempted not to tell you, because I think it is more difficult to love well, and that is our calling. I'm not even sure if Jacob's Well is relevant, to be honest. In his book, *In the Name of Jesus*, Henri Nouwen actually lists relevance as one of the temptations we face, just as Jesus did when He was tempted in the desert. Like Jesus, I want to be obedient, and by the grace of God, I think we are—in the messed-up and chaotic way of people who follow Jesus Christ and His living Spirit. If you asked different people in our community the same question ("What makes Jacob's Well relevant?"), my guess is you would get a number of different answers. Relevance is such a tricky topic. Often we use the word "relevance" to describe a person or community's ability to keep pace with the vagaries and trends of popular culture, and while that is important and good, I don't believe it is enough. What I hope is that you would hear a lot about love, and more importantly, that you would experience it within our life together and want to join us.

"WHEN I WAS YOUNG, CHURCH FELT LIKE A RESPONSIBILITY, LIKE MY PAPER ROUTE. I DIDN'T WANT TO GET UP AND DO IT, BUT I KNEW PEOPLE WERE DEPENDING ON ME. BUT AFTER COLLEGE, GOD'S WORDS TO ME THROUGH THE BIBLE AND OTHER BELIEVERS BECAME AN INTEGRAL PART OF MY LIFE. TODAY, EVEN IF I'M STRUGGLING WITH DOUBT, THE CHURCH IS A PLACE I KNOW I WILL GROW IN MY UNDERSTANDING OF THE HUMAN CONDITION AND MY NEED FOR SALVATION."

–ERIC RIDDIOUGH
ROSEVILLE, CALIFORNIA,
AGE TWENTY-NINE

THE NEW CHURCH:
ARTISTIC, MONASTIC, AND COMMUTE-FREE
BY KAREN WARD

BACK WHEN I WAS LIVING IN CHICAGO, I WAS LEADING a double-life. At age twenty-five, I was ordained, and I served my first church in inner city Philadelphia. In less than three years as a pastor, I got a "call from Chicago" (our Lutheran church head-quarters) with an offer for a job in ecumenical affairs (a sort of denominational state department).

Like a bright eyed new recruit, excited that the "church structure wanted me," I packed my bags and headed to Chicago to take up my duties as a young Turk apprentice at my church's Trump Tower. Like a junior Condi Rice, I went to work each day wearing black pumps and a suit. I sat down in my ergo-swivel chair in my Dilbert issue cubicle, with my Palm Pilot in one hand and Steno pad in the other. Some told me I had arrived—a young church executive on duty in the bishop's court. I may indeed have arrived, but the most fun began when I went home.

After work, I would get on the L train and head home to my loft in my too-cool-for-words Bucktown/Wicker Park neighborhood. There, I'd throw off the pumps, toss the briefcase, put on my worn jeans, flea market leather jacket, and baseball cap, and head out on foot to the Map Room Pub on Hoyne and Armitage. The Map Room describes itself as a "traveler's tavern," and the motto on their wall says, "Don't be Lost."

"WE BECAME A QUASI-CHURCH COMMUNITY, JUST WITHOUT THE CHURCH. WE WERE A SPIRITUAL GATHERING OF FRIENDS, WITHOUT THE UNFRIENDLY CONFINES OF RELIGION."

I was a traveler of sorts, traveling from my church world to my "real" world each Tuesday night. Unlike the church headquarters, at the Map Room, most people were my age. International dinner night was where I met a majority of my friends. Here I could be me: jeans, baseball cap, and Pumas. Just me. In my real culture among my peers.

My friends were also young Turks in their fields. Almost everyone had a master's degree or higher. We had twentysomething physicists, engineers, computer geeks, University of Chicago Ph.D. candidates, and law students from Northwestern. We were an urban tribe in formation, and they appointed me as chief. The only real difference between me and my tribe was church. I belonged to one. My friends did not.

Not unaware of the irony, in many ways we became a quasi-church community, just without the church. We were a spiritual gathering of friends, without the unfriendly confines of religion.

When introducing me to a Tuesday newcomer, a friend would sometimes say: "Karen is our pastor, and we are her secular congregation." And if someone did not show at the pub for dinner, another friend would say, "Karen, one of your sheep is missing. Wanna borrow my cell?" My friends were always half joking of course, but half serious as well.

The harder part came with the spiritual discussions, as every so often, a spiritual conversation would surface real curiosity about church. As our gang's "pastor," I got asked on several occasions if I could recommend a church. But the problem was, I never could.

After some years of traveling between parallel universes (modern church world by day, postmodern friend world by night), the split really started to bother me.

Two things were true. My friends were young and spiritually open. My friends didn't go to church. And I totally understood why. If I hurried home from modern church world to postmodern friend world, I knew my friends could never be coaxed into making the reverse commute. At that moment of realization, my time of "cultural commuting" had to end, and my dream of starting a "commute-free" church, one where my friends could relate, was just beginning.

During my Dilbert days in Chicago, I traveled to Seattle many times on church-related work trips, and on one such trip, a friend drove me into a funky urban neighborhood of Fremont. That evening, we went to a place called The Triangle Pub, and when I saw how packed it was with urban young adults, just like my friends in Chicago, I knew right away this was home.

Two years after that trip, a Lutheran bishop in Seattle who was crazy enough to authorize a Gen X church plant offered me a ticket to follow my God crazed dream.

So there I was, back in Fremont, the Bucktown/Wicker Park of Seattle. This was an urban artistic village that looked and smelled like home. And sure enough, the demographic studies confirmed that Fremont was young, well educated, artistic, 70 percent single, and X.

"MANY CHURCHES STILL ACT LIKE MISSION IS SOMETHING DONE OVERSEAS AND LIKE AMERICA IS A CHRISTIAN NATION."

So I knew in my heart that Fremont was be the place to hub a new commute-free mission. Ironically, just a year before I came, the one Lutheran church in Fremont had closed, leaving only one remaining church in a vibrant, young adult neighborhood of eighteen thousand people. *How whacked is this*, I thought. Young adults are literally falling from the trees here.

Although the church had closed, God's arms were still wide open. So this was the place where I set up shop.

LIFE @ THE CENTER OF THE UNIVERSE

Many churches still act like mission is something done overseas and like America is a Christian nation. Well, whoever thinks that has never spent much time in Seattle.

People in Seattle like their coffee strong and their espresso stronger. Beer is micro-brewed and hopped. No one carries an umbrella. Gortex is the native fabric. Jeans with holes are the standard dress. Jeans without holes are formal wear. The Subaru is the car of choice. Backpacks are the local briefcases. Trail mix is the local snack, and "none" is the local religion. (Literally, in polls and surveys, when asked to check a box to represent their religion, none is the majority option in Seattle).

Fremont is an urban village that calls itself both "a people's republic" and "the center of the universe." Ground zero (since the 1960s) for Seattle's counter-culture, Fremont is proud of being quirky, unconventional, artistic, and free-range. Whatever rules and social conventions apply elsewhere don't apply in Fremont, since this place is "a state of mind."

At the center of the universe, people express their spirituality by artistic creativity and observing the rhythms of nature. Art is so prevalent that Fremonters meet and navigate in relation to landmarks of public art, and nature spirituality is so pervasive that people tell time according to a schedule of nature festivals.

The Fremont Troll is a massive concrete sculpture under the Fremont Bridge. The troll is kept company by a giant statue of Lenin (imported from eastern Europe), a twenty-foot-tall aluminum rocket, and a human-sized sculpture of commuters "Waiting for the Interurban."

In Fremont, time is not solar but lunar. Local holy-day observances are not for Christmas, All Saints, and Easter, but for May Day, the summer solstice, and winter equinox.

Welcome to the center of the universe. This is my community, and I love it. Troll, rocket, Lenin, and all. Life here is buddahful, and mission is a high-wire, commute-free adventure where we build the plane as we fly it.

AN ARTISTIC CO-OP FOR THE SOUL

Despite being skeptical of organized religion, people here in general and young adults in particular have a hunger and thirst for God and spirituality. Even though 90 percent of those under forty here do not attend church, more than 80 percent believe in God, and almost 70 percent pray on a daily basis. So what gives? Somewhere and somehow in the eyes of many young adults, church is viewed as almost the opposite of spirituality, so much so that people are deeply aware that they are spiritual, but they can't see how the Church is spiritual, and how being part of a church can help them with their spirituality.

Part of the reason the culture does not find spirituality in the Church is probably because the Church does not find spirituality in the Church, much less spirituality in the culture. So to begin bridging the spirituality gap with culture, we start, not with speaking, but with listening, and not by preaching, but by being. We listen to people and take them at their word that they are spiritual.

"IN THE EYES OF MANY YOUNG ADULTS, CHURCH IS VIEWED AS ALMOST THE OPPOSITE OF SPIRITUALITY."

Because of this, we can focus our energy not on judging the spirituality of others, but on nurturing our spiritual community. We drink deep from the rich liturgical traditions of our Lutheran and Anglican tribes in combination with an expansive use of multimedia and the creative arts. Far from seeing culture as lacking spirituality, we see culture as brimming with spirituality and creativity that reflects the Creator. So our thing is not to try to download spirituality into unspiritual people, but to help nurture the spirituality each person has toward God-directed expressions.

When new folk come to our community, they become part of an artistic Christ co-op for the postmodern soul. Everyone is an artist, because we all are "God's workmanship, created for good works in Christ." Our gallery is our world. Our canvases are our lives in service to God. The brushes are our talents, gifts, and creativity. The paint is the Gospel. The inspiration for the art of life comes from the Spirit.

Currently we hold our weekly worship (Saturdays at 5 p.m.) at the corner of 43rd and Fremont Avenue in a former hair salon. The exterior windows are decorated with exploding dog cartoons. The interior walls are painted blood red. We sit on white Ikea chairs, accented by opium den pillows, a big purple sofa, and a plush purple chair. African drums line the walls. The altar is a café table draped with Pier One fabrics and Martha Stewart sheets. The pulpit is a music stand.

Our liturgy has been described by visitors as "new wave Byzantine" and "digital Orthodox." We are liturgical and sacramental. Communion is weekly. We are ancient and future. We Bach and rock. We chant and spin. We emo and alt. We are a CCM-free zone.

We write our own church music and incorporate mainstream music as well—everything from Rachel's to U2, Björk to Moby, Dave Matthews to Coldplay. We have no need to "Christianize" music. God is sovereign, and the whole world is God's, so any music that is good already belongs to God.

We have DJs and turntables, taggers and spray paint, emcees and poets. We have our own iconographers. We have a ministry of making our own Anglican prayer beads and cards. We are nu monastics—urban, postmodern monks. Our community is our priory. And since most monasteries have guesthouses as an open door to the world, our storefront is our guesthouse.

EXPLORING CHURCH WITHOUT ONE

In Seattle, most people are wary of churches. In Fremont, people are downright allergic, so Apostles is trying to be church without having one. Our storefront is called Living:room. It is not a church. We are the Church. On Saturdays at 5 p.m., Living:room (the tea bar) hosts Apostles (the church). Our candles and homemade icons are brought out to adorn our worship. After service, they are returned to storage, and Living:room morphs back into its weekday mode as a neighborhood net lounge, tea bar, art house, and music joint.

After one and a half years of existence as an urban spiritual co-op and nu monastic community, I'm beginning to come to the conclusion that if postmodern generations don't relate to modern churches, it is probably for good reason.

In the modern era, church had become removed from real life and distant from real culture, ignoring real spirituality for institutional religion. And many postmoderns (like my friends) have been unwilling or unable to commute. But now that there are more emerging missional communities, many don't have to.

"IN SEATTLE, MOST PEOPLE ARE WARY OF CHURCHES. IN FREMONT, PEOPLE ARE DOWNRIGHT ALLERGIC, SO APOSTLES IS TRYING TO BE CHURCH WITHOUT HAVING ONE."

As far as I know, Jesus did not ask His disciples to run modern churches or make cultural commutes. He did ask them to love God above all things, to love their neighbors as themselves, and to go make disciples.

It feels good to not run a church and to pastor a missional community instead and operate an Internet tea bar on the side. We love God and love our neighbors. We love mentoring new postmodern disciples and forming new urban monks.

Apostles is our priory and Living:room is our guesthouse. Local artists have openings. Local poets slam. Local DJs spin. Local bands rock. We have sixty apostles, after starting with four. I'm in my jeans, wearing my cap, sipping my tea, and surfing the 'net. One of my non-church friends from Chicago (who recently moved here) loves the place. And so do I, 'cause I don't commute.

> **"THE CHURCH IS MY FAMILY, MORE THAN MY ACTUAL FAMILY HAS EVER BEEN."**
>
> **—ADAM HEARE**
> PAMPA, TEXAS, AGE TWENTY-FIVE

10

THE DEATH OF
COOL

BY TODD SPITZER

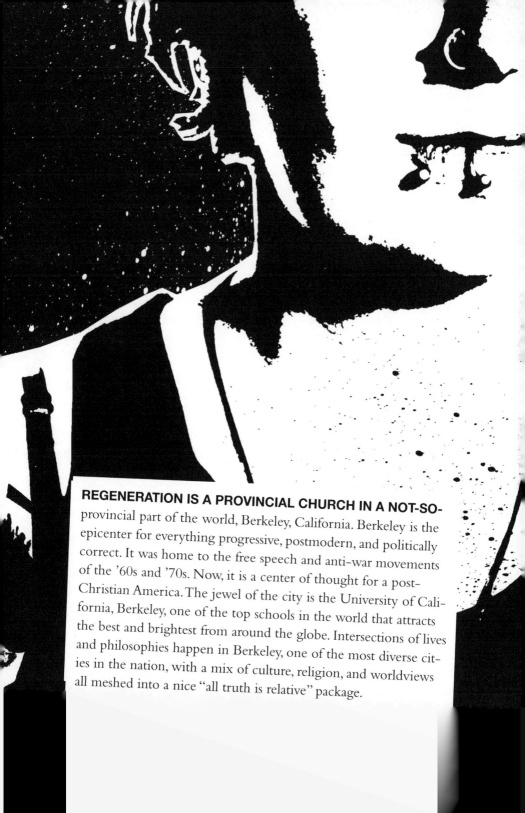

REGENERATION IS A PROVINCIAL CHURCH IN A NOT-SO-
provincial part of the world, Berkeley, California. Berkeley is the
epicenter for everything progressive, postmodern, and politically
correct. It was home to the free speech and anti-war movements
of the '60s and '70s. Now, it is a center of thought for a post-
Christian America. The jewel of the city is the University of California, Berkeley, one of the top schools in the world that attracts
the best and brightest from around the globe. Intersections of lives
and philosophies happen in Berkeley, one of the most diverse cities in the nation, with a mix of culture, religion, and worldviews
all meshed into a nice "all truth is relative" package.

It is here in Berkeley that Regeneration has thrived in what up until recently has been a ministry graveyard. Just like the culture outside our doors, our church is a community of diversity. Some were raised in the Church, and others never thought they would set foot inside of one. Some went through the turbulent '60s, and others weren't even born yet. Asian, European, African. Liberal and conservative, affluent and homeless. Coming simply as they are, they enter through the doors for our Sunday evening services.

The draw? It's not about our space. We once met in a dilapidated nightclub with black walls and a disco ball. We now meet in an old austere Seventh Day Adventist church, complete with blue shag and matching pews. The choice of environment, groovy or stale, didn't change our original purpose for people to connect with the truth of who God really is.

"THE DRAW? IT'S NOT ABOUT OUR SPACE. IT'S NOT EVEN BECAUSE WE HAVE GREAT COFFEE AND SOY PRODUCTS."

It's not just because we have talented musicians and artistic worship expression. Those times when we scale it all back to a guy and a guitar, the worship seems to be more.

It's not even because we have great coffee and soy products.

Sure, these aspects of Regeneration may help to remove the stigma often associated with the cold, detached, and archaic aesthetics of liturgy. But it's not the coffee, couches, or candles that draw people to our church, nor is it that we look to the latest ministry model or what's hot off of the Christian cultural press. We're not purpose driven, seeker friendly, or postmodern in our style or approach. In fact, we consider ourselves po-mo-phobic.

So what caused our church to thrive in Berkeley, California? It's the same reason why churches thrived in Corinth, Ephesus, and Rome. And that is by declaring the whole counsel of God found in the Scriptures (Acts 20:27). The truth of God's Word scratched on parchments so long ago, these reveal the true beauty of God, for they hold in them the greatest and most relevant message of all: the message of the cross. It's the cross that gives Regeneration the power to be cross-cultural and cross-generational.

We are all empty and need to be filled with what is real and life giving. With this inherent longing to fill this emptiness, even the most unlikely people come to our gathering because they are searching for meaning and purpose—the most basic need of the human spirit. Let me tell you about Ken, someone who deeply experienced the pit of destitution. Our church first met Ken when he was living outside with countless other homeless people at People's Park. Ken was without a job, estranged from his family, had no home or income, and felt alone and empty as he struggled with an addiction. A group from our church that spends time at People's Park invited Ken to our Sunday evening gathering, and there, the Word of God started to penetrate his heart. He was also given a tape player, as well as our Bible exposition teaching tapes, from which he would voraciously listen to five or six messages a day.

As the Word went in, transformation took place. The emptiness was filled with the knowledge of who God is and how much He loved Ken. Soon, Ken was no longer bound by his addiction. He was off the street in his own apartment, he started a job, and he began a restoration process with his family. More than that, as Ken was washed by the Word, he started to serve in the church and to help others he knew in the park who were without hope to see a glimpse of the hope and the truth of God found in His Word. We used to call him "Homeless Ken," and now we call him "Ken-ya!" since he's about to participate on our missionary trip to Kenya, just one of many ways that God has transformed and filled his life, such that it is now an outpouring of God's grace and love to others.

Seeing how God revealed Himself to Ken reminds us that the answer we seek about being relevant isn't on the horizon, nor is it found in the latest doctrinal fad or ministry model. It is found in the past. I think of the story in Genesis 26 in which during a time of drought and famine, Isaac went to the valley of Gehor. He went to the old wells that his father Abraham had dug and found them filled in with dirt by the Philistines. Isaac dug the wells out, and he and his family were refreshed, not by digging a new well, but by returning to the old well that had been clogged up with the dirt of the Philistines.

What we need is not some new truth or understanding, but a return to the old truths that have been there since the beginning. A return to that which we once believed. Re-digging the source of refreshment that has been filled in over the ages either by the enemies of the faith or by those in the faith who have opted for a cultural Christianity over a biblical one.

Digging in other wells or digging new wells that are promoted by the world as life-sustaining only leaves one dry and thirsty. Angelina was searching for intimacy and tried digging in many wells that seemed to hold promises—empty promises. She always knew God existed, and she tried to chase for a deeper truth by praying to God through Catholicism and Buddhism, as well as practicing witchcraft and taking crystal meth as she danced away at raves. Still empty and longing, she even experimented with being intimate with other girls. There was no peace.

"THE REALITY IS THAT IT ISN'T ABOUT REGENERATION. GOD'S WORD IS RELEVANT, NOT OUR WORDS ABOUT GOD'S WORD, AND IT IS GOD'S SPIRIT THAT TRANSFORMS THE HEART OF A PERSON."

Angelina found her way to the Bible study we were doing in the early days. As the Scriptures were taught, she drank of the well of the living water and discovered God and the intimacy He truly offers for herself.

After fully understanding the intimate love of God, she was able to say, "I am nothing without Him. I love the Lord with all my heart. He is my Father and Savior!"

"AS THE SCRIPTURES ARE TAUGHT, RELEVANT CHANGE HAPPENS, BECAUSE GOD'S WORD DOES NOT RETURN VOID."

At Regeneration, we seek to re-dig the old wells of the fathers in this time of spiritual drought and bring the refreshment found in the Scriptures to a new generation. We preach Jesus Christ and Him crucified. We teach with the simple expository teaching of the complete revelation of truth in the Bible, from Genesis to Revelation, the beginning to the end and everything in between. As the Apostle Peter penned so poignantly, "All things that pertain to life and godliness are found in the word."

As the Scriptures are taught, relevant change happens, because God's Word does not return void. This was seen in our humble beginnings as a Bible study. A handful of us once met in the back room of Mocha Lisa, a favorite coffee house on College Avenue in Berkeley. We were separated from the main seating area by a thick velvet curtain, but every week when we concluded our study, we'd pull back the curtain to find that people had inched their seats closer to eavesdrop on what was happening behind the curtain. Perhaps initially they were simply curious. Once they strained their ears above the noise of the coffee grinders to realize that the Scripture was being expounded upon, they didn't pull away and refocus their attention on their cappuccinos. Rather, they were drawn to who God is as revealed in His Word. Many were refugees from religion and tried to run from a cultural god by hiding out in Berkeley, and others would never associate themselves with church or Christianity. Yet in these conversations that were overheard, stereotypes were torn down as His love by the cross was taught to show the true and living God. Hearts were softened and lives were changed—God's Word does not return void. Our Bible study grew, reached capacity, burst, and became a church.

Now, our church reaches out to the homeless who amass at People's Park and to the runaways and gutter punks who sit in hopelessness along Telegraph Avenue. Many engage the street philosophers of Sproul Plaza on the UC Berkeley campus, and many sing to the forgotten in convalescent homes.

Regeneration extends beyond Berkeley as well. Our church helped create ROHI, a children's home in AIDS stricken Kenya. We planted and currently sustain a church in Elista, Russia, which is located in the backwaters of central Asia. We also help the indigenous tribes of the Guayme in Panama receive the Bible in their own language so they may more directly see and experience the refreshment found in the Scriptures.

We have members in the arts and in all professions, all engaging culture without needing a five-point formula to do so. How? By living out what they have learned in God's Word. No gimmick, no pretense. Just simple and true.

"I DON'T THINK PASTORS OR CHURCH LEADERS NEED TO BE RELEVANT. I THINK GOD IS BEAUTIFUL ENOUGH ON HIS OWN."

The reality is that it isn't about Regeneration. God's Word is relevant, not our words about God's Word, and it is God's Spirit that transforms the heart of a person. God's Word tells us that the Scriptures are the very breath of God (2 Timothy 3:16) and they are is so important that He exalts them even above His own name (Psalm 138:2). David tells us to meditate on it day and night (Psalm 1:2). Why? As the Apostle Paul tells us, it has the ability to transform lives (Romans 12:1-2). It is living, active, powerful, and piercing (Hebrews 4:12). God's Word is a shield, a hiding place, a light revealing direction. It brings hope, builds faith, and breaks addictions. It heals, it teaches, it guides, and it gives life. Jesus said in the Gospel of John that God's Word is truth—and it's the truth so many are longing and searching for.

Jesus said we are to be in the world and not of it, but now all too often, the Church in America is of the world and not in it. The Church, in her desire to be relatable, has become popular to the masses through concession and compromise. Her cry has been, "Away with those songs about the blood of Jesus. Let's not talk about unpopular topics like repentance and sacrifice. You need to quote Kurt Cobain instead, if you really want to make a point. And the Word of God? That's boring and archaic. Let's replace all of that with positive stories or movie clips, and then we can make some hip analogies like 'take the red pill, man.' Let's dress God up to make Him attractive and lovely because He's not on His own. Let's make Him in our image so He will be as popular as us—postmodern, hip, and trendy!"

It's a sad state that so much of Christianity is in today—a Laodicean laxity. A sickening spirituality. A church with Jesus locked outside, pounding on the door. So many of us make Him sick with our selfishness and self-sufficiency when we only look to our own methods or worldly ideas of how to be relevant while ignoring His.

The cure is simple and yet profound: Teach the truth of God's Word and see regeneration occur as God's Word reveals to us who God is, how much He loves us, and that He died for us. He will impact your community with the greatest message the world has ever heard, a message just as relevant today as it was when Jesus first crashed into history.

"WHEN I HEAR THE WORD 'CHURCH,' I CRINGE. IN A SUPPOSEDLY HIP NEW CONGREGATION, I WAS TAKEN OUT OF LEADERSHIP BECAUSE I DIED MY HAIR AN UNNATURAL COLOR AND PIERCED MY NOSE. THAT WAS FOUR YEARS AGO, AND I HAVEN'T BEEN PART OF A CHURCH SINCE. I'M STILL A FIRM BELIEVER IN CHRIST AND HAVE A STRONG RELATIONSHIP WITH HIM. HIS LOVE FOR AND ACCEPTANCE OF ME HAS LITERALLY BEEN THE ONLY THING TO KEEP ME ALIVE AT TIMES. IT MAKES ME SAD THAT I CAN'T FIND A CHURCH THAT TRULY UNDERSTANDS CHRIST'S LOVE AND ACCEPTANCE."

—RENEE CLAY
BIRMINGHAM, ALABAMA, AGE TWENTY-FIVE

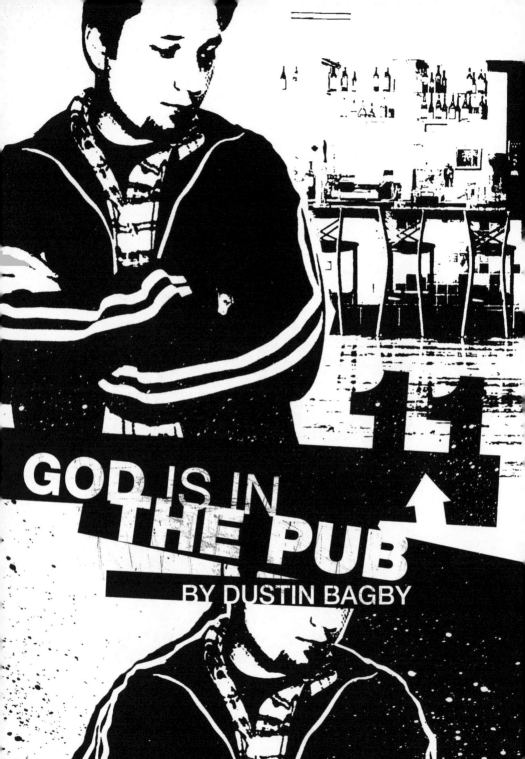

GOD IS IN THE PUB

BY DUSTIN BAGBY

I MET JULIO AFTER ENROLLING IN AN EIGHT-WEEK stand-up comedy class at a popular club in New York City. After the final session, I invited him to our small group, and now he attends on a regular basis. Julio feels perfectly comfortable as a part of our small group, but he hasn't come close to a Sunday service, even though he grew up Catholic.

I can understand many reasons those in their twenties are not interested in church. After all, I am only twenty-four myself. If I weren't a pastor at Mosaic in Manhattan, I think church would have a hard time catching my interest at times. At this age, we are seeking our own identities, career paths, and life companions. What a confusing time of life! Now, on top of that, throw in the

Church. Many would find church to be a place that helps with identity and relational issues, but the truth is, most twentysomethings are not going to enter a church—at least, not through the front doors of a "church" building. Why? How can we share Christ's love and design for life if people my age never step through our doors?

I think people in their twenties don't attend a church regularly because they don't see the life-changing power of God through the Church's expression of forgiveness, grace, love, acceptance, and passion. This is nothing new; the same thing happened in Ezekiel's day. "You don't build up the weak ones, heal the sick, doctor the injured, go after the strays, look for the lost, you bully and badger them. And now they're scattered every which way" (Ezekiel 34:1-6 The Message).

Julio, my friend from stand-up, was going to become a godfather, so he was forced to go back to church. He was actually excited for the push, because he had a desire to get his life straight and thought attending church would be the place to do just that. I met him for lunch after his return from church, and he told me, "I was thinking that the Church was going to be excited because their prodigal son came home. I was expecting a party and celebration. What I got was a lecture of all the things I need to do now that I was back at church and a guilt trip for being away so long."

What a sad time when a person cannot return to church and experience God's heart in the place where His Body resides.

People in their twenties are looking for something that demands their whole lives from them. They are looking for a God in whom they can find identity and a purpose for living. They are hungry to hear who God is, what God wants from them, what God has done for them. They are hungry to study Scripture in depth. As the Church, we have done a good job of being practical and relating a majority of topics to everyday life, but in the process, we have left the spirituality and the mystery of faith people so badly desire somewhere far behind. Those seeking God typically attend church to seek God, not to hear a year's worth of "how-to" seminars.

Josh is a twenty-four-year-old with whom I grew up in a small town. After graduating college, I moved to New York City, and Josh moved to Chicago. He came to visit me for a week over Thanksgiving. One night as we sat down at a pub in Greenwich Village, he told me something very surprising.

"Dustin, I really want to be a Christian and please God with my life, but I don't know how. None of my friends go to church. I don't even have a Bible, but I really need something more out of life. I just feel like my life is worthless right now. Can you help me?"

"I THINK PEOPLE IN THEIR TWENTIES DON'T ATTEND A CHURCH REGULARLY BECAUSE THEY DON'T SEE THE LIFE-CHANGING POWER OF GOD THROUGH THE CHURCH'S EXPRESSION OF FORGIVENESS, GRACE, LOVE, ACCEPTANCE, AND PASSION."

After this conversation, Josh attended a small church near Chicago.

"I was hoping to get something awesome, but what they talked about was how the Church needed to stay strong with all that is happening in the world and addressed problems with ministers and elders. There was nothing really about following Jesus. For a newcomer, I was completely turned off and left with the same unquenched desire to know God."

It is said that in the Paleolithic Age (five million to ten thousand BCE), art was a form of prayer. Art was one of the most ancient ways humans tried to engage superhuman forces to advance human needs and efforts. Ritual prayer usually required the proper combination of words (chanted, sung, or spoken), visual images, and gestures (perhaps a dance). We need to go back to the very beginning of time in this present day and worship God with the creativity with which He deserves to be worshiped in our services and in our culture. At Mosaic, we have a high value of the arts. We believe that God created us to be creative ourselves.

Here are a few things we have done that may be relevant for your community. We host a monthly Art Expression Evening, a Midweek Music Jam, comedy nights, and an Open Mic Night (scary, but can be fun if it's done right). For more ideas, try looking at what other people in the creative arts or what other churches are doing creatively. Don't be afraid to ask them for permission to do the same thing. Creative ideas are meant to be shared.

"WE NEED TO WORSHIP GOD WITH THE CREATIVITY HE DESERVES ... AT MOSAIC, WE HAVE A HIGH VALUE OF THE ARTS. WE BELIEVE THAT GOD CREATED US TO BE CREATIVE."

But let me give you a warning about creativity. Many times when churches try to be creative, they tend to fall heavily on the side of performance and production. You don't need to be a performance-based church to be creative. You can truly be creative and interactive at the same time. When twentysomethings are seeking God, the last thing they want is a flashy production that doesn't portray real life and an honest view of spirituality.

One Sunday, we passed out a blank sheet of paper as people came in and set up three canvases in the front of the auditorium. During the message, we asked people to draw a picture of how they would express spiritual growth and asked three volunteers to come forward to the canvases and paint their expression. Art coaches were at the easels to help if the person so desired it. The art coaches could guide and give advice to the people painting, but they could not do any actual painting. This is how we illustrated whether or not we use the resources that are available to us to grow.

At the end of another service, we had each person take a puzzle piece as they left and asked them to bring it back the following Sunday. The next week, we had everyone who brought it back turn in their pieces and then put the puzzle together. There were several pieces of this puzzle missing, and we used this to illustrate the fact that as a church, we need each person to complete this mosaic called God's kingdom. What we do creatively is usually simple, and many times we borrow the idea from someone else. These creative elements can include dance, poetry, comedy, video, painting, sculpture, and anything we can think of to engage people's senses.

To make an impact in the twentysomething culture, leaders need to be involved in "real" culture, not just Christian "subculture" events. If you are a musician, then you should be in the music clubs performing on weekends, not just at Christian coffeehouses. If you are a comedian, you should be working in the comedy clubs during the week as a way of meeting people and impacting the community. If you are an athlete, join a league and play with a random group of people, not just a church league. We encourage people to use their gifts not just "in here," but "out there."

Unfortunately, many people who have grown up in church were taught to avoid culture at all costs. They were taught that we need to form an environment in which to live and then invite other people to join. The problem is that the people who we are inviting to join are not coming. Now it is time to go "out there" and meet them. I find that most of Jesus' teachings are about going and harvesting. I hear very little about sitting back at an event and hoping people who are not followers will attend. Jesus always went to where the people in need were.

We need to stop inviting people to Christian events as our only form of outreach. Instead, start inviting people to spend time where they already are. There is a choice to be made here. We can either try to bring a person into our setting—however uncomfortable they may feel—or we can spend time with an individual in their setting and sacrifice our comfort. You will find people respecting your effort to get to know them on their turf. This makes the process of getting involved in a church much less intimidating (whether the person is a follower or not) simply because of the relationship and trust that has developed.

For years, we have had an evangelical mindset that says, "We need to create a cool event that non-Christians will come to. Then we can invite a bunch of non-Christians and share the message on our turf, where we feel most comfortable." Instead, if we are going to reach people who are not comfortable walking into a church service on a Sunday, we need to start thinking, "Who can I invite to grab dinner tonight? Who can I invite to a rock show? Who can I invite to a movie? Who can I invite to grab a bite to eat after work?" These are the places where life transformations that many of us have been missing out on can take place. Cool programs will never do what time with people in a neutral or even an intimidating (for us) environment will do.

Kurt Powers, the former lead singer of the band Time Flies, said, "I love this church. I've never been to a church where my pastors would come and hang out with me at rock shows, the bar, and my apartment before." Kurt has recently made the decision to stay in New York City after being offered a job in L.A. where he would make more money, where he would have a much bigger apartment at half the cost, and where his wife Heidi could go back to school. Why did he do this? "I've never been to a church where we've really felt like we fit in like this before." Let me make sure you understand that it is nothing Mosaic does in their service specifically that would make Kurt say this. What makes Kurt and Heidi stick around are the relationships.

For this reason, we have started a Theology Pub. A church called Spirit Garage was doing this very thing as a way to discuss theology in contemporary culture in a casual atmosphere that would allow participation from everyone. The people we want to come to Theology Pub are individuals who might never step in the doors of a Sunday service as their first point of entry. For these people, it will take time and trust to attend anything that has to do with Mosaic specifically.

"WE TRY TO 'HAVE CHURCH' FIVE OR SIX DAYS A WEEK JUST BY SPENDING TIME WITH PEOPLE, ASKING CHALLENGING QUESTIONS OF THEM, ENCOURAGING, ACCEPTING, AND LOVING BOTH THOSE WHO KNOW CHRIST AND THOSE WHO DON'T."

I would like to tell you more about our service, but as good as I feel it is, I don't believe our service is what is most effective or even what we do best. I believe what happens on the other six days are an equally important part of church. We try to "have church" five or six days a week just by spending time with people, challenging, asking questions, encouraging, accepting, and loving both those who know Christ and those who do not.

The story with Josh did not end after that night at the pub. We began reading the Bible together and discussing what we read every Sunday on the phone. I remember one Sunday in particular when Josh said, "I couldn't wait for the day when I could call you and tell you that I'd crossed over into faith." I couldn't wait for that day either. I honestly thought it would take some time, but when God is working in someone's life, it's hard to resist Him for long. Josh called two days later and said, "Guess what, Dustin?"

Josh probably never would have stepped through the doors of a church by himself, not until one thing happened—a relationship.

The most appealing part of our service isn't our service; it's the people who are having "church" every night in homes, at rock shows, in bars, at dinner, and everywhere in between. Until we recognize this as being just as valid as a Sunday service, we will not impact our generation.

"THERE ARE SO MANY THINGS I LIKE ABOUT CHURCH. I LIKE PRAYING WITH OTHER PEOPLE. I LIKE DIFFERENT STYLES OF THEOLOGY AND PRACTICE. I LIKE WATCHING EVERYBODY'S KIDS RUN AROUND AFTER THE SERVICE. AND I LIKE THE OLD PEOPLE—THEY'VE WEATHERED SO MUCH, BUT HAVE HELD ONTO THEIR FAITH AND STILL HAVE A LEVEL OF SPUNK AND HUMILITY THAT GIVES ME HOPE FOR WHAT I CAN BECOME.

BUT THEN AGAIN, THERE'S THINGS I WISH DIDN'T EXIST IN THE CHURCH— THE SEXISM, OR THE WAY THE CHURCH ADAPTS SECULAR CULTURE AND ADDS A CHRISTIAN SPIN TO IT. AND I ESPECIALLY DON'T LIKE HOW MONO-CULTURAL SO MANY CHURCHES BECOME, FAILING TO BE A HOME TO THE DIVERSITY OF THE NEIGHBORHOOD IN WHICH THEY GATHER."

—UNA LUCEY
PASADENA, CALIFORNIA, AGE THIRTY-FIVE

12

BEING THE CHURCH vs. GOING TO CHURCH

BY JASON ZAHARIADES

I'M AMAZED AT HOW BIG THE WORD "CHURCH" IS.
If we gathered ten people together and asked them, "What is the Church?" we would probably end up with twelve to fifteen definitions. One might associate the word with a small local church on the corner. Another might equate it with a large mega-church. Another might remember a mission organization or a home Bible study. One might think of a youth group, while another might think about a benevolence program or twelve-step program. Another might even picture a famous or influential pastor in the pulpit. Still another might associate church with a particular style of music or liturgy or doctrine or denomination. One person may imagine an intimate community of friends, while another may think about evangelism, while still another might think about a discipleship program.

Whew! It's amazing how one little word can be so packed with differing images and meanings. But with two thousand years of history behind us, could we expect any less?

However, when we define Church as a place we visit, a program we attend, a pastor we follow, or by our personal preferences, I believe we miss God's intentions, because, at its core, the Church is none of these things. The Church is God's people.

There's an old Sunday school rhyme, accompanied with hand motions, that goes like this: "Here's the church/ Here's the steeple/ Open the door, and here's all the people."

But that's an incorrect view of the Church. The rhyme should go something like this: "Here's the building/ Here's the steeple/ Open the door, and here's the CHURCH."

Okay, it doesn't rhyme very well, but at least it's theologically correct. The Church is the people of God. We don't go to church. We are the Church. We don't have church. We are the Church. We aren't even Pastor So-And-So's church. We are God's people. It's been my experience that when we forget this basic truth and operate as if the Church were something else, then a lot of bad things happen.

I've been a professional pastor for sixteen years. I've seen the Church do a lot of good. But I've also seen—and to my shame, participated in—the "dark underbelly" of Church as well. We've all heard similar horror stories—the church split over the color of the carpet, the fight in the church parking lot over a parking space, the firing of church staff because a leader feels threatened. There's been judgment, gossip, embezzlement, affairs. You name it.

Check this out. The other day as I was leaving Taco Bell after another occasion of fine dining, some lady yelled at me from her car, blocked my car in its stall as I was trying to leave, and flipped me off. I was completed taken aback when I then watched her drive out of the parking lot and turn into the Christian bookstore down the street (hopefully to find a book on anger management).

I believe a lot of the pain and grief caused by many churchgoers and even church-leaders is because we operate from an incorrect perspective of the Church. Dallas Willard has said we are at the mercy of our thoughts. If we embrace a false perspective of Church, it will ultimately lead us to a false experience as the Church.

The Bible offers a captivating perspective on the Church. Two thousand years ago, Jesus said to a small group of God's people, "I will build my Church." In other words, the Church belongs to God, and He has eternal designs for His people that are relevant and meaningful today in our lives, families, employment, neighborhoods, and networks.

"WHEN WE DEFINE CHURCH AS A PLACE WE VISIT, A PROGRAM WE ATTEND, A PASTOR WE FOLLOW, OR BY OUR PERSONAL PREFERENCES, I BELIEVE WE MISS GOD'S INTENTIONS. THE CHURCH IS GOD'S PEOPLE."

It's taken me nineteen years of walking with Jesus to realize something: The key to acquiring and cultivating a proper vision of the Church is to explore its place within the sweeping Story of God, in which Jesus and His earliest followers lived. It's a story that begins with creation and finds its ultimate fulfillment as a new creation—the new heaven and new earth (Revelation 21:1).

GOD'S STORY

In the beginning of the Story, God creates the cosmos as a dynamic and ever-growing expression of His love and goodness. Within this vast array of goodness, God forms humans in His image to govern creation properly under His good leadership. By maturing into God's character through an intimate and dependent relationship with Him, humans would create and nurture goodness from the raw materials within creation.

It's interesting to note the importance of human community in the opening chapters of God's Story. At each point in the creation process, God affirms His approval by stating, "It is good." However, when God sees Adam alone, there is a stunning declaration, "It is not good for the man to be alone" (Genesis 2:18). Adam's solitude is the only aspect of God's creation that is not good. Creation finally becomes fully good when God forms human community, of which marriage is the most intimate expression.

"IF WE EMBRACE A FALSE PERSPECTIVE OF CHURCH, IT WILL ULTIMATELY LEAD US TO A FALSE EXPERIENCE AS THE CHURCH."

However, the first humans attempt to become like God on their terms. Pursuing an alternate course of independence and self-will, they plunge creation and humanity on a trajectory of corruptibility, violence, alienation, and death.

Yet, God is not thwarted. Generations later, He calls Abram to be the progenitor of a new nation—a nation God would bless so that it could then bless the other nations. This nation, Israel, would be God's chosen people, a specially equipped resistance movement in the midst of a corrupted world. Blessed with God's presence, Spirit, and Word, this unique community would enjoy an intimate and dependent relationship with God, allowing them to cooperate with Him in re-creating this broken world back toward God's goodness. And through the community of Israel, God would ultimately deal with the problem of Adam's sin.

Yet, over its long history, Israel distorts its vocation as a blessing to the nations. Rather than being an inclusive transformative community, it accentuates its distinct ethnic identity in order to keep the other nations at bay.

Again, God's plan is not impeded. At the proper time, God sends His Son. Born fully human and into Israel, Jesus embodies God's full life and presence on earth. He simultaneously demonstrates what the human race was intended to be and what Israel as God's chosen people were intended to be. In other words, Jesus is the climax of both human history and Israel's history. He shows us how to be truly human and how to be truly God's people.

Jesus climaxes God's Story by inaugurating God's future kingdom in the present. This was the good news Jesus proclaimed: "The kingdom of God is near" (Mark 1:15). In other words, God's future new creation, the finality of God's Story that we anticipate at the end of time, has begun in the present. Through His entire life—His birth, teaching, ministry, crucifixion, resurrection, and ascension—Jesus embodies God's future new creation, inviting everyone to join Him and to share in this new life. By trusting and following Jesus, anyone can learn from Jesus how to live his or her life fully in God's future kingdom now, just like Jesus did (Matthew 11:28-30). We can become by grace what Jesus is by nature—truly human and truly God's people. As God's people, we are a community that is to increasingly embody God's fullness and kingdom in our daily lives for the sake of the world. This is the Church that Jesus is building.

LIVING IN GOD'S STORY

Although climaxing with Jesus, God's Story doesn't end with Jesus. You and I, as the Church, are living smack-dab in the middle of this amazing Story. Eugene Petersen, author of The Message, tells of a time when his grandson climbed into his lap and said, "Grandpa, tell me a story and put me in it." Being God's people means living our lives in God's Story.

Have you ever used one of those directory maps at the mall? The thing that makes the map make sense is the little dot that says, "You are here." Knowing where you are is essential to knowing where you are going and how to get there. As humanity and creation are journeying toward the finality of God's new creation, the New Testament defines where we are and how to get where we are going.

In 2 Corinthians 5:17, Paul states, "Therefore, if anyone is in Christ, he is a new creation; the old has gone, the new has come!" Paul's choice of words is intentional. Anyone who is trusting and following Christ by learning from Him how to bring one's entire life into God's kingdom is a "new creation." With those words, Paul doesn't simply mean "brand new" or "has a fresh start." Rather, the person who has immersed his or her life into the One who fully embodied God's future new creation has become part of that future new creation as well. By doing this, we become a new kind of humanity.

"GOD'S WILL IS THAT THE CHURCH, GOD'S NEW HUMANITY, WOULD BE CONFORMED TO THE LIKENESS OF HIS SON. THIS IS HOW THE NEW CREATION IS BIRTHED."

With that in mind, let's look at Romans 8. Paul spends the first seventeen verses discussing the difference between being a new kind humanity (living by the Spirit) versus being the old kind of humanity (living by the flesh). Paul then moves in an astonishing direction. God's people actually living as a new kind of humanity according to the Spirit has direct implications upon present creation's transformation into the new creation.

In Romans 8:19-22, Paul states: "The creation waits in eager expectation for the sons of God to be revealed. For the creation was subjected to frustration, not by its own choice, but by the will of the one who subjected it, in hope that the creation itself will be liberated from its bondage to decay and brought into the glorious freedom of the children of God. We know that the whole creation has been groaning as in the pains of childbirth right up to the present time."

Notice, creation is longing for God's people to finally be revealed in their full glory as the sons of God and co-heirs with Christ (c.f. Romans 8:17). When this happens, creation will be brought into the liberation enjoyed by fully realized children of God. New creation is being born in God's people, and the entire creation is groaning in the birth process.

Now look at Romans 8:23: "Not only so, but we ourselves, who have the first fruits of the Spirit, groan inwardly as we wait eagerly for our adoption as sons, the redemption of our bodies."

Not only is creation groaning for the birth of the new creation, but so are God's people. We who have the Spirit and live by the Spirit as God's new humanity begun in Christ also groan for the final birth of God's new creation.

Now Romans 8:26-27: "In the same way, the Spirit helps us in our weakness. We do not know what we ought to pray for, but the Spirit himself intercedes for us with groans that words cannot express. And he who searches our hearts knows the mind of the Spirit, because the Spirit intercedes for the saints in accordance with God's will."

We discover that the very Spirit who dwells in us is groaning for the birth of the new creation as well. But the Spirit's groaning is intercession for the saints in accordance with God's will. What is God's will?

Look at Romans 8:28-29: "And we know that in all things God works for the good of those who love him, who have been called according to his purpose. For those God foreknew he also predestined to be conformed to the likeness of his Son, that he might be the firstborn among many brothers."

This is where it all comes together. God's will is that the Church, God's new humanity, would be conformed to the likeness of his Son. This is how the new creation is birthed.

New Testament scholar N.T.Wright likens this passage to Russian Babushka dolls.These are the kind of dolls that upon opening one doll, you find another.You then open that doll to find another, and so on. Each doll is embedded within another.

God's Spirit, who is striving for the new creation, is embedded within the Church. As we live according to the Spirit, we bring our lives and longings into synchronization with the Spirit and find His inward momentum and power toward the goal of Christ-likeness. Christ-likeness is the new creation in human form. As the Church intentionally journeys toward Christ-likeness in the Spirit, it finds itself embedded within broken creation. So as we live by the order of God's new creation in our families, jobs, schools, neighborhoods, and relationships, we progressively cooperate with God in the transforming or re-creating of creation into the new creation. In other words, the Spirit draws God's people toward the new creation, and God's people draw the rest of creation in the same direction.

A COMMUNITY OF NEW HUMANITY

But what does the life of the new creation look like in human form? Two statements by Jesus can unpack it for us.The first is Matthew 18:20. Jesus says: "For where two or three come together in my name, there am I with them."

In the Bible, one's name is intimately connected with one's character or nature.The life of the new humanity occurs when two or more come together as Jesus' apprentices, learning to live like Him as the embodiment of God's fullness and kingdom.When we do this, Jesus is present.We incarnate Him as a community of loving apprentices. We experience Christ's life and presence within the communal life of Christ's apprentices who come together in Christ's nature.

A second statement Jesus makes in Matthew 28:18-20 takes us further:

"All authority in heaven and on earth has been given to me. Therefore go and make disciples of all nations, baptizing them in the name of the Father and of the Son and of the Holy Spirit, and teaching them to obey everything I have commanded you. And surely I am with you always, to the very end of the age."

The Church is not only a community of Jesus' apprentices who are blessed with His presence. Like Israel, we are blessed in order to be a blessing to others. That blessing occurs when we help others join God's new humanity by entering life in God's kingdom as Jesus' apprentices. Again, this was the good news Jesus proclaimed.

The plan is simple. We come together as Jesus' apprentices learning to become by grace what Christ is by nature. This community is then blessed with Christ's presence, the full incarnation of the Trinitarian God. By bringing people into this community, we baptize or immerse them into the nature and reality of the Trinitarian God, who is love.

Within this loving incarnational community, Jesus' apprentices are progressively taught the means to actually obey everything Jesus commanded. This is essential, since John states, "If anyone obeys his word, God's love is truly made complete in him. This is how we know we are in him: Whoever claims to live in him must walk as Jesus did" (1 John 2:5-6). In other words, we are learning to become the kind of love that God is.

And fully behind this plan is Christ Himself, who wields all the authority in heaven and earth to accomplish His Father's will of a new creation in and through His people.

So this is who we are as the Church, as God's people. We are a community of people who are following Jesus into His likeness as God's new humanity. Indwelt and empowered by God's Spirit, we progress together in grace toward the likeness of Christ and thus continue the incarnation of God's fullness and kingdom in the world as Jesus did.

Being embedded within creation, our incarnational communal life as Jesus' apprentices cooperates with God in the re-creating of this world toward God's new creation.

66 CHURCH IS NOT JUST A BUILDING OR SUNDAY MORNING SERVICE, BUT A PLACE WHERE THE BODY OF CHRIST COMES TOGETHER FOR ENCOURAGEMENT, EDIFICATION, CHALLENGING, REBUKING. IT'S A PLACE WHERE PEOPLE ARE CARED FOR, A DWELLING PLACE OF THE HOLY SPIRIT, AND A PLACE OF WORSHIP. **99**

— CORY PASSEHL
TOWNSVILLE, AUSTRALIA,
AGE TWENTY-EIGHT

13

CONNECT, EXPERIENCE, LIVE

BY HOLLY RANKIN ZAHER

I WOULD'VE LAUGHED OUT LOUD IF SOMEONE WOULD'VE told me ten years ago that I'd be planting a church with Don and Shannon Cox. Ten years ago, Don was the most amazing middle school youth minister I knew. He gave me the best advice for working with middle schoolers I had ever heard: run and scream. Since then, Don and Shannon had spent time as missionaries in Mexico. Don's funny. I mean, really inappropriately funny. He intentionally spends time trying to get under my skin like my brothers used to. And he's successful at that.

Ten years ago, I had no aspirations of being a church planter or even being a "planter partner," the term Don and Shannon use to describe the part my husband Jim and I play in our church plant, THREE-NAILS. I wanted to be a youth minister, and that in and of itself was a new dream to me. I wanted to change the world with all of my twenty-one-year-old enthusiasm. And I did, to some extent. I might not have cured world hunger, but the One I worship impacted lives. Sometime in my youth ministry career, something shifted for me. I returned back to my youth ministry job in Tallahassee from a Youth Specialties convention where I heard Dan Kimball speak about starting new services and church planting, and something clicked. I have been reading about our current culture shift for the past several years, and I wondered if planting a church might be the easiest way to engage the current culture instead of trying to change an existing church structure. It was a nice, clear autumn day as I left church that Sunday morning when I caught up with the pastor, a good friend and mentor. As the sun poked through the trees, we talked briefly about these ideas. His immediate acceptance and enthusiasm caught my attention—my mind raced with possibilities.

"BEING A NEW CHURCH ENTITY, OUR STRUCTURES AREN'T FORMED, AND WE ARE STILL FIGURING BASIC IDEAS OF WHO WE ARE AND WHO WE WANT TO BE AND TO BECOME."

A few months later, Don Cox called me and reminded me of a desire that we had to work together. We prayed and checked out some church planting opportunities, but dead ends popped up at every turn. Still, the idea of working in community with people I knew and trusted continued to grow stronger.

I met Don and Shannon when I was doing the Josiah Project, a collegiate leadership development program sponsored by Rock the World Youth Mission Alliance (*www.rocktheworld.org*). The year after I completed the Josiah Project, I signed up for another of Rock the World's training programs, their Student Ministry Professional Program, which trained youth ministers. Don was also in that program.

It was during that time that I remember first meeting Dan, a high school student. One of the middle schoolers from the church I served had a mad crush on him—Dan was a student in leadership at a retreat and a year older than she. I had the privilege of desperately trying to get Dan, who was learning how to play drums, to keep in time when I led musical worship for our favorite coffee house—that was a painful experience!

Little did I know that one day we'd all be on the same church planting team.

I've kept in touch with Dan, Don, and Shannon over the years, especially at ministry events where Rock the World alums led retreats and conferences. It is so easy to do ministry with people who have the same DNA—that notion of deeply following Jesus, a value on Scripture, the option to risk at times and be free to fail in order to create, and the ministry of all people—whether old or young or male or female. These values allowed us freedom when we worked together. Rock the World and the Episcopal Diocese of Pittsburgh offered Don and Shannon the job as church planters to plant a church in Pittsburgh in the emerging context. It wasn't a surprise to me when Don popped his head into my office and asked if I would be on board. Don worked hard over the next few months to recruit a team, one that included more than eighty percent of people who had previous involvement with Rock the World. Dan was also among the original team gathering in the spring of 2004.

It's strange to me to be writing about THREENAILS. We are in such flux! Being a new church entity, our structures aren't formed, and we are still figuring basic ideas of who we are and who we want to be and to become. We had our first public (read: not in a house) worship gathering just last week. It was amazing.

The rented art gallery was full of music. Ceramics on pedestals dotted the floor. As I set up, I had a flashback to eighth grade. (I accidentally knocked over a Precious Moments figurine in a Hallmark store and did not have the money to pay for it!) "Be careful moving these chairs," I reminded myself as I set up the station for praying through Scripture in the back corner. Nestled behind a pillar, this station allowed for some amount of privacy, a contemplative feel in a busy place. I welcomed people into the space and gave some options as to how they might engage and worship God. Many things were going on at once: songs and scriptures sung, a paint-by-numbers icon that introduced folks to praying through iconography, a video sermonette by Don that unfortunately no one could hear in this space where sound bounced around everywhere, a video projection unit showing slides focused on suffering, which was the topic of the evening. People milled about drinking coffee, admiring the ceramics, praying through Scripture in the back or with the icon in the front, still, dancing, and singing. At some point, Don, who is also an Episcopal priest, prayed over the bread and the wine so we as a community might eat in remembrance of Jesus. Then Dan led people through a basic contemplative exercise. All the while, others took advantage of the rest of the stations throughout the space. It was beautiful.

I honestly didn't think it was possible. My favorite phrase for our creative expression group, of which I was in charge, was that we were "trying to find our worshiping identity." Composed almost entirely of artists, trying to get our group to agree on much of anything was akin to herding cats. In our first meeting, we had some people saying things like, "I've never seen musical worship done when it wasn't manipulative or coercive, and I don't want any part of it," and the complete opposite perspective: "Musical worship is where I connect with God. It's where I catch a vision for how God sees me as His follower. It's how I worship."

Needless to say, the first meeting wasn't very promising.

The second meeting didn't go much better. We were at a great coffee shop only designated by a large lower-case "a" on the outside of the store. One of the guys had just brought in his new guitar to show it off—it was really nice! Folks in the shop asked us if we were a band. I tried to focus us on what we needed to do: plan a worship gathering. We kept slipping into the big questions of, "What was worship anyway?" and, "Can we even plan this when we have competing ideas of worship?" but I kept bringing us back to the task at hand, continually difficult to do since I would have much rather discussed the philosophical questions. I almost audibly growled when a discussion got underway about the use of video and movies and the philosophical underpinning of the decision. But plan we did.

"WE ARE STILL DISCOVERING OUR WORSHIPING IDENTITY AS A COMMUNITY. THE ONLY WAY TO DISCOVER IT IS TO TRY DIFFERENT WAYS OF DOING THINGS AND THEN HONE IN ON WHAT FEELS AUTHENTIC AND WHAT IS CONSISTENT WITH THE HISTORICITY OF THE CHURCH AND SCRIPTURE."

Two things were happening in our Creative Expression Group that mirrored what was going on in the rest of THREENAILS. One was that the group as a whole was deconstructing what they thought about worship, and more broadly, what they thought about church. So much of what we were doing as a community was challenging all known ideas of ecclesiology. In Rock the World culture, worship was akin to music. These folks were coming of age and asking difficult questions about the place of music in worship. We intentionally called this musical worship instead of deeming it "worship," which suggests that everything else is "not worship." I like to ask questions and get people to think, so my tactic has been to be patient and work through these issues because they're important. And our willingness to deal with the form and function of church, especially in a liturgical tradition, I believed, in the end, would make or break THREENAILS. In many ways, I have felt like the pastor of deconstruction over the past year, my time with the Creative Expression Group illustrating this perfectly.

Secondly, a fear gripped most of the members of THREENAILS: What if we fail? What if we are not good enough? What if we are not cool enough? Do we really know how to craft a worship gathering in such a way that folks who are not following Jesus might understand and grasp what is going on? We didn't want to just do what everyone else was doing. I finally called us on our fear and challenged us to take a step. We intentionally have been rotating leadership of our worship gatherings so that we do not unintentionally sign off on a certain "form" of our corporate worship gatherings without agreement from everyone in THREENAILS. Like I said before, we are still discovering our worshiping identity as a community. The only way to discover it is to try different ways of doing things and then hone in on what feels authentic to us and, for us, is consistent with the historicity of the Church and Scripture.

"NESTLED BEHIND A PILLAR, THIS STATION ALLOWED FOR SOME AMOUNT OF PRIVACY, A CONTEMPLATIVE FEEL IN A BUSY PLACE. I WELCOMED PEOPLE INTO THE SPACE AND GAVE SOME OPTIONS AS TO HOW THEY MIGHT ENGAGE AND WORSHIP GOD."

Our last worship gathering was made possible by our leadership cluster, the leadership arm of THREENAILS. We have a dream team of young leaders. Don meets with each person of the leadership cluster every other week for mentoring meetings or situational coaching. Don describes these times: "I'm a friend, a spiritual director, someone who holds people accountable to their lifestyle, and tour-guide on this journey: whatever the situation calls for." Don sees this as a way to illustrate that we all are on a journey, and he is just walking alongside. Together, they can look for road signs that might help in determining where they are. Every person who meets with Don crafts a rule of life that enables him or her to live a balanced life. Don illustrates this in his own life by talking about the things he does to care for himself (Don to Don), to care for his wife, to care for his family, to care for his life as a follower, and to care for his life as a church planter. Don models this by going out of his way to walk alongside folks in THREENAILS.

On top of a rule of life, Don asks each person to embark on a personal project. Dan emailed me a few months ago asking for links about contemplative prayer for his personal project that he is doing with Don. By exploring different ways of praying, Dan discovered a Jesuit site that has been teaching him the ways of contemplative prayer. Dan, in turn, is teaching this to others. It is so exciting to see Dan catch a vision of being a learner, not just in doing ministry, but also in his own spiritual life as well.

"Dynamics of a Jesus movement" and "using a missiological lens" are phrases that you would hear a lot in THREENAILS, especially at City Fellowship, the model leadership cell. As a cell-based church, we are made up of a number of different cells all throughout the city of Pittsburgh. There, time is spent in Scripture developing a philosophy of ministry, looking at the people movements of Luke and Acts. Our goal is to be authentically following Jesus in our own particular context and have authentic and real relationships with others. To do this, the City Fellowship continually attempts to separate form from function. City Fellowship is not so much interested in models and more interested in what God is calling us to do and be together.

"CONNECT, EXPERIENCE, LIVE: THOSE THREE WORDS DESCRIBE THREENAILS MORE THAN ANY OTHER."

Our cell group consists of five married couples, a young, single man and woman, and several kiddos from the ages of two to fourteen. We gather almost every Friday night for a meal and to hang out. A few weeks ago, I was incredibly tired as we finished up dinner at 9 p.m.

I knew there was no way I'd be able to last for our typical discussion, prayer, and communion. I suggested to my husband that we go home. The rest of the group invited us to stay and for me to take my first trimester pregnant self and sleep on the couch. Here I was, with everyone else around me sharing and praying, all curled up so comfortable that I managed to not only fall asleep, but to drool as well. I have never been encouraged to sleep in the middle of church before, and our cell was such an encouragement to me as a newly pregnant woman who was realizing her limitations!

Connect, experience, live: Those three words describe THREENAILS more than any other. Through this process, all involved are attempting to connect (ourselves and others) to the heart of God, experience real relationships with real people, and live life together transforming our world. I have no idea what THREENAILS will look like in five years, much less in the next year. What I do know is that this adventure of planting a church with Don and Shannon Cox and the rest of the leadership cluster has been a wild ride on which I've been changed, hopefully to look more like the One we follow and worship.

" CHURCH IS THE ONE PLACE WHERE I AM ACCEPTED 'AS IS.' CHURCH GIVES ME AN UNDERSTANDING OF HUMAN FRAILTY AND REMINDS ME THAT WE ALL NEED GOD'S FORGIVENESS—EVEN ME. GROWING UP AS A REFORMED JEW, I WAS ALWAYS PRESSED TO ACHIEVE AND COMPETE. THEN WHEN I BEGAN ATTENDING A CHRISTIAN CHURCH IN COLLEGE, I DISCOVERED CHURCH COULD BE A PLACE OF AMAZING REFUGE, ACCEPTANCE, AND SALVATION. "

—JENDI REITER
NORTHAMPTON, MASSACHUSETTS;
AGE THIRTY

14

A WEEK IN THE LIFE OF A MISSIONAL COMMUNITY

BY MARK SCANDRETTE

IS CHURCH RELEVANT TO THE PERSON LIVING IN AN
increasingly complex, mobile, and pluralistic society? It depends
on how we understand "church" and what it means to live as
followers of Jesus. Notions of church simply as a religious institution, building, or weekly worship and teaching event appeal to a
consumer and cognitive approach to spiritual life. Christian faith
reduced to belief statements and political affiliation betrays the
hunger we feel when we hear the Nazarene say, "I have come
that they may have life to the full." For anyone who has heard the
stories of the Gospels or read accounts of the lives of early "Christians," it is hard to reconcile the revolutionary, subversive, and supernatural dynamic of these companions with what most people
today picture when they hear the words "Christian" or "Church."
And yet if we can imagine a more passionate, integrated, and soul-

ful way of life in Jesus, we can also seek to live as pilgrims in search of such a way. We may find that the best way to be relevant is to be irrelevantly consumed with loving the Creator and creation. We might also discover that this living way is more a quest than a destination. What I can contribute to this conversation about church is my own pilgrimage toward a communal way of life in Jesus. I offer an account of one week in my life in the context of my family, October 5-11, 2003. Through this narrative I hope to reveal something of my struggles and hopes to live in the story of God with others. Included are some of my reflections and observations along the way.

SUNDAY OCTOBER 5, 2003.

I jump off the subway train at the Oakland Coliseum Station and hop on an airport shuttle for my 2:30 flight to L.A. Vietnamese sandwich in hand, I sit down to catch my breath. I've come from East Oakland, where I help lead a spiritual community for second generation Mien and Cambodian students. These are the children of people who escaped Cambodia and Laos by boat, or somehow survived the killing fields of Pol Pot. An aged and fading urban church sponsors me to do this work and to lead services for a small elderly congregation. We are a curious group that gathers to pray, sing hymns, and discuss the Bible: my wife Lisa and I, a homeless man, a retired atomic physicist and his wife, two younger women from the housing projects, a matronly upper class Armenian widow, a zealous apocalyptic fundamentalist hairdresser, a Chinese-American school teacher, a thirteen-year-old El Salvadorian boy, his older sister who just graduated pre-med from Berkeley, and anyone else who happens to walk in off the street.

I often ask myself why I am involved in such a quirky old school church institution. It's not sexy or hip, and almost everything about it defies my personal sensibilities—especially considering that I see church more as something we are—a people seeking a way of life in Jesus—and not a building, an event, or particular rituals. My church is everyone in my relational and spatial proximity who also aspires to be a follower of the Way. So why am I here? 1) I have respect for these older people who have labored for twenty years to serve and empower struggling refugee immigrants in East Oakland. 2) I see that Jesus cares about aliens, widows, and orphans, and I want to as well. 3) We want our kids to know people who have roots in other languages and places. 4) I feel I can be of some use here teaching about the way of Jesus, and 5) for now, it's part of how I pay for unexpected car repairs and braces for two kids.

"I OFTEN ASK MYSELF WHY I AM INVOLVED IN SUCH A QUIRKY OLD-SCHOOL CHURCH INSTITUTION. IT'S NOT SEXY OR HIP, AND ALMOST EVERYTHING ABOUT IT DEFIES MY PERSONAL SENSIBILITIES."

At the airport, I brush the bread crumbs off my suit and head through security. I'm all dressed up for John and Becky's wedding. On the plane, I sip coffee, nibble dark chocolate, and read a bit of Walker Percy's novel *The Thanatos Syndrome*. My mind wanders to the friends I will see at the wedding.

Brian, John, and I met five years ago at an event in Santa Fe, New Mexico. With common activist tendencies, we instantly connected in our dreams to discover a more organic form of spiritual community. We were also captured by the revolutionary invitation of Jesus into a new way to be human. Brian and I had both worked as pastors, but quit our jobs to play with the idea of being missional communities and journeying toward a more integrative, sustainable, and holistic way of following Jesus.

The last time I saw John and Becky was last summer in Palm Springs, where John and I led a spiritual retreat for artists and musicians. John works as a mural artist. This wedding is going to be a kind of reunion for Icthus, a collective of friends in L.A. who sought the way of Jesus together for five years. They shared meals and faith practices in living rooms, started small businesses, and often lived together. Icthus had connections to the L.A. electronic music scene. Some people from the dance clubs found their way to Icthus and into a new experience of God. Our family traveled down to Pomona a few times to visit Icthus and to celebrate the achievements of Millennium Gallery, the art, poetry, and music lounge Icthus sponsored downtown. Friends from Icthus would come stay with us and help out with our events in San Francisco. We collaborated on an art and poetry happening called CONVERGENCE. We spent a week together picking up trash from the streets of our neighborhood and assembled the debris to create found object art—as a metaphor for the Creator's intention to remake us into the genesis vision of God. Food and drink, poetry and trance beats, art and conversation—one hundred twenty-five people packed into our little Victorian house in the Mission District that December night. We went on to collaborate with Icthus on other projects, including an international art-based worship experience in Austin, Texas, called EPICENTER.

For many of us, creativity has become an important way of nurturing relationships, experiencing God, exploring and integrating spiritual realities into the messiness of our lives. Through the creative process, we imagine what our lives were meant to be from the beginning.

Ryan pulls up to the airport in a white Mercedes Benz, on loan to him while he visits from Azerbaijan. We arrive at the winery two hours early. I stroll the grounds and give hugs and kisses to old friends. I hardly recognize Dylan, who looks so confident and healthy compared to three years ago when he came to Icthus clinically depressed. The groomsmen wear mullet wigs while having their pictures taken. Laughter fills the air as the sun fades in the West, and the wedding begins. Brian and Heidi officiate the ceremony together with tearful affection for John and Becky. Over the course of the evening, I catch up with about twenty people who were up in the mix of Icthus. I am introduced to new spouses, babies, and the parents I've heard so many stories about. We feast and dance late into the night. Eventually, Brian and I sit down to catch up on the twists and turns our lives have taken over the past year.

After Icthus disbanded, he and Heidi and their two kids moved to Venice Beach, where Brian reads screenplays for a production company and works as an art director on feature films.

"CREATIVITY HAS BECOME AN IMPORTANT WAY OF NURTURING RELATIONSHIPS, EXPERIENCING GOD, EXPLORING AND INTEGRATING SPIRITUAL REALITIES INTO THE MESSINESS OF OUR LIVES."

The warmth and love at this wedding is evidence of how transformational friendships can be. Some of the best intentional efforts at community making are temporary. With Icthus, people came together at a critical time in their lives, learned important lessons, and are now finding their way in the world and becoming what they were made to be. The life of Icthus, as an organic urban tribe, continues without explicit structure. I believe this level of tribal community is only possible for people who have an internal orientation toward relationships and engaged spiritual exploration. In other words, it's not something that can be programmed. I sense that the common criticisms about "church" are related to the tendency in our culture to become too dependent on large institutions to broker relationships and manage our personal chaos. Institutions, programs, and structures ultimately disappoint when we expect them to do what we were made to do for ourselves: inhabit and make a life together in the rhythm of God.

MONDAY OCTOBER 6, 2003.

After the wedding, a bunch of us crash on the floor at Paul and Kieva's. I awake early to a quiet house and slip out the back door to read a Psalm and write. Elijah and Jeremiah, Paul and Kieva's sons, come out to show me their backyard toys. Over coffee and breakfast, Brian shows us the trailer from an Italian film he just finished working on. We pray for one another, holding hands in a circle of blessing. Ryan and I depart, steering north up the coast of California on Highway 1. Among our friends, hospitality is seen as elemental to a new way life.

We have people stay over at our house thirty or forty times a year and share meals with others two or three times a week. I see many people longing for "community," not realizing that deepening supportive friendships can take years to cultivate. There is no instant formula for significant generative friendships.

On the road, we listen to live tracks by a techno percussionist Ryan heard last year in Istanbul. He tells me stories about his life in Azerbaijan, where he is learning the language with hopes of starting sustainable businesses. We make little stops to take pictures or pick up coffee in Ventura, Morro Bay, and San Simeon. Over the course of the day, we cover the familiar interior territory: our personal recovery and identity issues, perspectives on how best to move through the world in the rhythm of the Creator, and our learning about various cultures and peoples. Walking on the beach in Santa Barbara, we discuss the psychology of our families of origin and have an animated conversation about some of our theological differences.

"TOGETHER WE'VE BEEN PART OF A LABORATORY COLLECTIVE CALLED REIMAGINE! EXPLORING WHAT IT MEANS TO BELIEVE AND PRACTICE THE WAY OF JESUS IN AN EMERGING WORLD URBAN LANDSCAPE."

I form the closest relationships with people who are in pursuit of similar dreams. I like to think that what we share is a desire for the realization of a genesis vision of God. With my friends, there is a growing sense of a common life, similar values, and practices—and a conviction that we were made to help make the world a better place.

We reach Big Sur just before sunset and grab our cameras to take pictures of Pacific cliffs and flying sea gulls. The sky is misty and cool. As the full moon rises east inland, Ryan wanders off to read and pray. I walk along a trail filled with gratefulness to be road tripping with a friend in such a gorgeous place.

For me, being out in nature is an act of worship. I feel God's presence most in natural environments. I am moved by the sight of the ocean, force of wind, and sensation of sand between my toes. The elements speak of the reality of God and act as a spontaneous prompt for gratitude.

Up the road, we find a rustic candle lit inn and stop for dinner. We order a bottle of California Syrah, goat cheese and greens, roast duck and yams, a dark chocolate raspberry tort, and coffee. It is a day to splurge and celebrate friendship, beauty, and the abundance of the Creator. "But, what would make this day perfect," I say, "is a soak in a hot tub." Our server tells us that the only tubs available are a mile up the road at an exclusive resort. "If you walk in like you belong, they won't mind."

It's eleven o'clock, and Ryan is driving up the road. We pass a security guard sitting in a truck who follows us up to the guest parking lot. "We don't have to do this, Ryan," I say. Opening his car door, Ryan replies, "Let's keep going until we come to a closed door." I follow him up to the guest entrance. Inside the doors, we are greeted by two security guards chatting. We say hello, walk cautiously through the lobby, and realize we have no idea where we are going. Through a maze of well appointed sitting areas, we find a back door and walk out in search of Japanese tubs. My heart is beating fast. Up the hill we find the tubs. We are alone on a mountain overlooking the Pacific Ocean. There are fresh towels and lemon water, and we ease into the steaming tubs—a bit giddy with the novelty of our situation.

Even though our actions may seem questionable, I believe this type of risk taking reveals my personal quest to develop an experimental approach to life, as well as how friendship gives a person greater courage.

An hour later, we walk back to the car and drive down the mountain. We park along the road and lay out sleeping bags at the edge of a two-hundred-foot cliff descending into the ocean. Often awakened by the pounding waves and the brightness of a full moon, I lay awake much of the night meditating and praying.

That night I felt like I experienced a measure of what St. John of the Cross called the "Dark Night of The Soul." I find myself increasingly drawn to contemplative practices: spiritual retreats, contemplative prayer, quiet walks alone, silence and solitude. These activities help me integrate what I know cognitively from years of reading Scripture into the experiential fabric of my daily life.

TUESDAY OCTOBER 7, 2003.

I sleep until 8:30, and we continue up the coast. By 10 a.m. we reach the white sand beaches of Carmel by the Sea. Ryan jumps in the waves, and I go for a run along the shore. After a stop at my favorite French bakery in Carmel, we speed through San Jose and Palo Alto and spend our last hour on the road praying for one other.

Back in San Francisco, I hop on my bike and ride through the Mission up to the Lower Haight District. I'm meeting Linda, Dieter, and Kenny at Squat and Gobble Café to make final preparations for an event we are hosting together this weekend called EQUILIBRIUM: Life with God in the New Reality.

Together we've been part of a laboratory collective called ReIMAG-INE! exploring what it means to believe and practice the way of Jesus in an emerging world urban landscape. We've shared life in each other's homes, banged on drums and worshiped with our children, wrestled with Scripture, and feasted with the homeless.

Later in the afternoon, I catch up with Lisa and our kids. Noah (eight), just back from photography class, is excited about develop-ing and enlarging his own prints. Hailey (nine) reads me a short story she's been working on and tells me about an opportunity she has to audition for a role in an independent film. Isaiah (seven) tells me a joke and shows me a Lego ship he's working on. We wrestle on the floor, tickle, fight, and tell stories about the last two days. Soon Mer-edith and Aurora come up from their apartment downstairs to meet Ryan, and we make plans to go out for dinner together. Meredith came to California last year to sort out some things from her child-hood and to be near our family. Aurora fell in love with San Francisco and moved from Seattle last month.

Many of us look forward to the freedom of living outside a house-hold, released from the expectations of and obligations to other people. Ironically, during this same stage of life, we often hunger for more significant relationships and accountability. For me, our family and our household is the most basic form of Christian community. It is the place where real formation and transformation happen. Lisa and our children know me when I'm crabby dad, critical husband, or wounded soul. I am what I am with them. There is no pretend-ing to be someone else. I believe we are placed among the people in our lives—extended family, roommates, coworkers, neighbors, and friends—in order to learn how to love. And isn't love what we were made for?

On a foggy night, we zip down Sixth Street to the best and cheap-est French Vietnamese food in San Francisco. A small plaque on the door declares chef Julia Child once ate here. Tulan Restaurant is in the SOMA sandwiched between check cashing places, porn shops, and liquor stores. Crack addicts scream and beg for spare change outside where we wait for a table for seven. Soon we are seated, and our table is filled with spicy plates of spring rolls, curry, shrimp salad, rice, chicken, beef, pork, and Vietnamese iced coffees.

Asceticism is a common human religious impulse that makes bodily pleasure the unqualified enemy of the spirit. Embracing the good-ness of creation has been a significant part of my soul recovery. Eating, for me, has become a central and sensory act of communal worship. The wise king Solomon once said that, if a person lives right with God, they are able to find pleasure in their food, their work, and their relationships.

After breakfast with the family, I take a subway train to Pleasant Hill station. An hour later, Floyd is looking at me intently, ready to listen to me talk about my life and what God might be trying to say to me. I'm sitting in a comfortable chair surrounded by shelves of books in Floyd's home office. Floyd, a retired pastor, is my spiritual director, and I meet with him once a month. Today we cover familiar themes: questions I have about my vocation, busyness, the insecurities and weak ego that drive me to hurry and perform, my tendency to escape into illicit sexual fantasies when I'm tired or stressed, longings I have to be more centered and grounded, the growth I want to see in my marriage.

A spiritual director helps a person listen to the voice of God speaking through the events and circumstances of life, connecting the realities of Scripture to the particularities of daily life. At a time when religious experience is often commodified and franchised, the art and practice of spiritual direction provides a personalized approach to spiritual formation. People who submit to spiritual direction are self-selected seekers, stepping beyond the crowded marketplace of mere curiosity to do serious and joyful business with the divine. For the person who is hungry for God, yet skeptical of authoritarian institutions or religious dogma, spiritual direction may offer a hopeful alternative search path.

My neighbor Miles calls to tell me that the drug dealers on our corner verbally threatened him. Once the domain of Honduran organized crime, a Latin gang has recently taken control of the drug trade on our street. Every day a steady flow of heroin and crack addicted people arrive to make transactions outside the Taqueria next door. Miles has scheduled a special meeting with the police captain and narcotics officers next Tuesday to talk about our concerns.

We believe that Jesus invites us to be healers, putting the broken pieces of the world back together. For our family, this means living in a particular neighborhood where we are close to poverty, addiction, sex trade, gunfire, and violence. We also get to meet amazing and interesting people from all over the world and taste the variety of God's character revealed through the art, music, cuisine, and traditions of many cultures. Place has become an important aspect of our spiritual journeying.

Tonight Meredith watches the kids so that Lisa and I can go out on a date. We walk down Valencia Street, stopping at a thrift shop and a couple of used bookstores, ending up at a café in the Castro for dessert. Our conversation orients around our desire to simplify life and develop a common rhythm of work, rest, play, service, and relationships. We discuss scheduling issues, decisions about kids' activities, household organization, and our personal development goals. At home with candles lit and the smooth sound of Astrid Gilberto's Bosa Nova vocals playing softly, we complete the day in sweet embrace.

THURSDAY OCTOBER 9, 2003.

I lock my bike on Fillmore Street and walk into the café for the weekly breakfast of the Dumb Fools. My friend Michael, an independent filmmaker, is already seated next to Darren. George, who manages a nonprofit, and Stephan, a photo-based artist, come in with their bike helmets and bags. I'm surprised to see Wally here because he recently moved back to Sacramento. There is the usual round of handshakes and hugs. David, a painter and writer, plops down and passes out copies of the poem he's been working on. "Read this," he says. "What do you think? Are you feelin' it?" After the usual banter about movies, art exhibits, and in-laws, we go around and share our highs and lows of the week: a new girlfriend, someone's search for a job, marriage difficulties, victories over a controlling behavior, grieving a recent miscarriage, balancing creative ambitions with the financial responsibilities of being a husband and father.

The Dumb Fools evolved from an artist collective we started a few years ago called THE BOON PROJECT. We did a series of community art shows and installations and fixed up an old warehouse to use as studio and gallery space. One winter we met together as a creativity recovery group, sharing meals and discussing personal disciplines and the integration of creativity and Christian spirituality. Some of us started going out for breakfast once a week to discuss art making, books, (principally Thomas Merton's writing), and our quest for an integrated life of faith. We needed a group where we could bring the mess and magic of what we are becoming. The name, Dumb Fools, is derived from a story I retold one day from the Little Flowers of St. Francis. Once when Francis felt he was becoming prideful about his piety and acclaim, he had his companions walk over his face repeating, "Francis, you are a miserable sinner in need of God's grace." Steven jokingly suggested that we call each other something derogatory, and the name stuck. No matter who I am in any other setting, these guys keep me real. Here I feel loved and known.

"I BELIEVE WE ARE PLACED AMONG THE PEOPLE IN OUR LIVES— EXTENDED FAMILY, ROOMMATES, COWORKERS, NEIGHBORS, AND FRIENDS—IN ORDER TO LEARN HOW TO LOVE. AND ISN'T LOVE WHAT WE WERE MADE FOR?"

I'm on my bike when Doug calls from Minneapolis to talk about a gathering we're planning in New Mexico in two weeks. Doug and I are part of an international network of leaders and faith communities called Emergent. Every couple of months we seem to hop on planes and meet in another strange city to plan or run an Emergent event. Although Doug lives two thousand miles away, he is part of my journeying community. Because of the mobility and complexity of contemporary society, I think it is most appropriate to see "church" as a multi-portal community—a network or web of all relationships and activities, both local and global, in which I share kingdom vision, values, and practices. We are the peculiar people of God wherever we seek the kingdom of God together.

Bernal Hill is a green area in the city just south of our house. Tonight the kids and I hike here for "Dad and Kid Night" while Lisa is out getting some personal time by herself. After dinner, we play a game of dinosaur monopoly and read a bit of the Bible together. I put the kids to bed and watch a film.

FRIDAY OCTOBER 10, 2003.

Today is our Sabbath. Noah and Isaiah and I get up early and go for a hike. Noah especially is a morning person, and our walk is filled with animated dialogue. Back at the house we grind coffee and make batter for whole wheat crepes. Darren and Pam and Jesse join us at nine o'clock for breakfast.

Usually we cook and eat together on Wednesday nights, but this week Pam had a San Francisco Orchestra Choral rehearsal. Darren and Pam are part of a Christian order among the poor working with homeless youth on Haight Street. Darren is also a writer. Living in a large city, people come and go a lot, and city people often find themselves cruising for better or more compatible friends among hundreds of acquaintances. Over a year ago, Darren and I decided to stop cruising and commit to a consistent friendship. We live in the same neighborhood, our wives get along, and we share some common interests. So our families have labored to knit our lives together. We eat together once a week, watch Jesse, take care of Peanut (their dog) when they are out of town, share cars when one of ours is broken down, celebrate holidays and birthdays together, and generally help each other out.

After breakfast, my mom calls to talk. She is recovering from cancer surgery and chemotherapy and is still wearing a wig. She and my dad are wrestling with the difficult decision of whether to place my grandpa in an assisted care facility while she continues treatment for cancer. Grandpa is needing more care than my mom can provide. We talk about this for a while.

After lunch, I take a two-hour nap. At 4 p.m., Darren picks me up, and we drive over to the Sam Wong Hotel in China Town to set up for EQUILIBRIUM. Some guests arrive early, and I grab Josh from Dallas, and we walk down the street to make dinner reservations. As we pop in and out of restaurants on Columbus, I find out more about Josh.

"BECAUSE OF THE MOBILITY AND COMPLEXITY OF CONTEMPORARY SOCIETY, IT'S MOST APPROPRIATE TO SEE 'CHURCH' AS A MULTI-PORTAL COMMUNITY—A WEB OF ALL THE RELATIONSHIPS AND ACTIVITIES, BOTH LOCAL AND GLOBAL, IN WHICH I SHARE KINGDOM VISION, VALUES, AND PRACTICES WITH OTHERS."

This weekend we've put together an opportunity to contemplate the realities of an emerging world and explore connections with historic Christian faith.

In our first session, Linda reads a quote from Descartes, and we discuss the implications of his philosophy on contemporary life and expressions of Christian faith. After the session, we walk down the street to Mona Lisa's restaurant in North Beach where we are served like kings and queens by men with thick Italian accents and bravado. We feast on bruschetta, montepulciano, pizzas, and pastas. Sean the Meat Head mystic and I ride back to our house with Steve and Michelle from San Diego, and we stay up way too late talking.

SATURDAY OCTOBER 11, 2003.

It is a cool foggy morning at the Botanical Gardens in Golden Gate Park. I read Psalm 104 to the group, talk about living in a God-bathed world, and encourage people to take an hour to walk in the garden and write poetry of awareness. An hour later, we walk through the rose garden to Dieter and Val's for breakfast. We share our poetry, and

Linda talks about the values of the deep ecology movement as an emerging cultural narrative. Dieter connects this with the holistic and integrative message Jesus proclaimed, "the kingdom of God is now available."

We eat lunch with twenty homeless neighbors at Page Street Community Center. I play guitar for a while with Johnson. While we're eating chicken and squash, Michael and I listen to Robert talk about the sexual abuse he survived that led him to life on the streets at age 15. He has a broad toothless smile.

We walk to an old firehouse that is now used as an art gallery, and I talk with the group about finding ourselves in the present reality of the kingdom of God. I describe Jesus as a Mystic, Healer, Artist, and Companion, and the invitation to become like Jesus through imagination, intentional practices, mindful awareness, and risk taking. David and I perform some spoken word pieces as a benediction to our twenty-four hours together.

Keith and Shane from Sacramento stay for dinner. We walk with my family down the street to a Thai restaurant. Our group sits outside in a private courtyard on a cool night, and we enjoy more conversation, jokes told by eight-year-olds, and tasty food.

At home, I help the kids settle into bed and make it an early night myself. Making a life starts again in the morning.

&& I KNOW THAT PEOPLE SAY THEY DON'T NEED CHURCH, BUT ANYTIME WE GATHER TOGETHER, GOD PROMISES TO BE WITH US. WHAT COULD BE MORE ENTICING THAN GOD'S PRESENCE? WHY WOULDN'T WE GO WHERE GOD PROMISES TO BE?**&&**

—ROBIN LEMKE
SEATTLE, WASHINGTON, AGE TWENTY-NINE

15

THE VALUE-DRIVEN CHURCH

BY MIKE HOWERTON

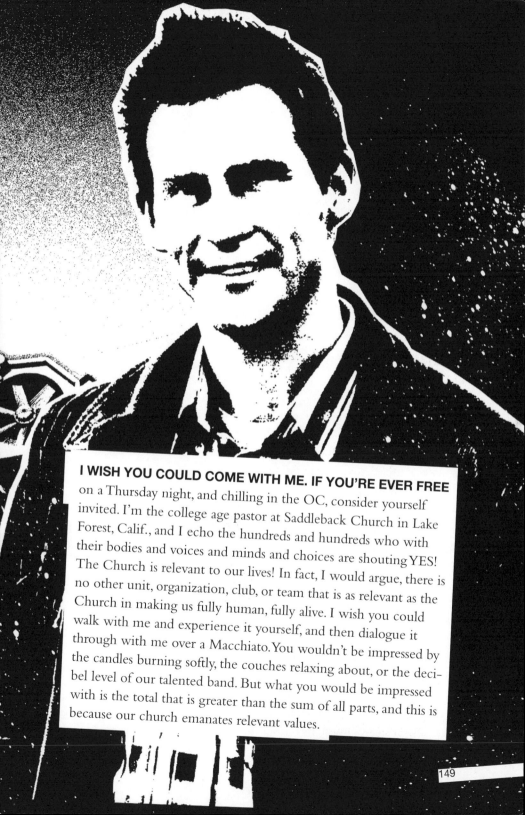

I WISH YOU COULD COME WITH ME. IF YOU'RE EVER FREE on a Thursday night, and chilling in the OC, consider yourself invited. I'm the college age pastor at Saddleback Church in Lake Forest, Calif., and I echo the hundreds and hundreds who with their bodies and voices and minds and choices are shouting YES! The Church is relevant to our lives! In fact, I would argue, there is no other unit, organization, club, or team that is as relevant as the Church in making us fully human, fully alive. I wish you could walk with me and experience it yourself, and then dialogue it through with me over a Macchiato. You wouldn't be impressed by the candles burning softly, the couches relaxing about, or the decibel level of our talented band. But what you would be impressed with is the total that is greater than the sum of all parts, and this is because our church emanates relevant values.

CRAVE is the name of our college age ministry, which gathers on Thursday nights.

Saddleback Church is a purpose-driven church, and CRAVE is a purpose-driven college ministry. The concept of "purpose-driven" has received much attention and is outlined in compelling books such as *Purpose-Driven Church* and *Purpose-Driven Life* (both by Rick Warren) and *Purpose-Driven Youth Ministry* (by Doug Fields). For more info, feel free to hit *www.purposedriven.com*. I know that God is blessing His Church as we become more and more committed to fulfilling the five purposes that He outlines in His Word.

"I WOULD ARGUE, THERE IS NO OTHER UNIT, ORGANIZATION, CLUB, OR TEAM THAT IS AS RELEVANT AS THE CHURCH IN MAKING US FULLY HUMAN, FULLY ALIVE."

But the unique way in which we fulfill God's purposes in this emerging generation is due to the fact that we also are value-driven. As we sought to connect on a large scale with the eighteen to twenty-four-year-old demographic, we realized pretty quickly that some screaming needs were readily apparent. We discovered these needs simply through dialogue—conversations again and again would center around these needs, and the more we watched these needs surface, the more we began to realize a cultural hemorrhage was erupting in front of us. Then we started to take a look at the media culture, and we realized that much of what the entertainment industry seeks to do is to fulfill these gaping and legitimate needs with cheap substitutes. This generation is quick to realize how cheap and shallow those substitutes are—and that disillusionment is one of the greatest opportunities for the Gospel I know.

Our values are developed simply as a response to those needs. We speak to these values in literally everything we attempt as a ministry. And the closer we come to hitting those needs, the more dynamically relevant our ministry becomes. Here are our values (and simultaneously the needs of our target demographic):

PASSION: Sustaining Purpose For Living

The dream of being a healthy human is stolen by our media culture, distorting and dehumanizing souls until women are good only in as much as they are sexy, and men are successful and strong or nothing at all. A good church articulates Christ giving the dream of living back.

The number one drive in our generation is a drive for passion. The allure of the rich and famous is the best the culture offers, and yet it is viewed and found wanting by this generation. The shell of passionless jobs, passionless marriages, the safe, the boring, the predictable, the empty—these pursuits are seriously being examined. The life that is being sought is a life of passion. A good church understands this, and embraces the passionate adventure that is a life lived with Jesus.

Dave Crowder sings, "Our love is loud," and it's true, but not only of our love and our music; everything about life and faith becomes grounded in a place of passionate intensity—it's all loud! This certainly doesn't mean intolerance, and it doesn't mean suicide bombing. Just the opposite: To truly love God means to love people, not causes. Passion is nothing more or less than a life lived in singular focus for that which is of utmost importance.

Every human on the planet is a worshiper; everyone worships something. We simply expose the latest idols, and we articulate the emptiness and dissatisfaction that comes from worshiping anything less than God. As a church community commits to embracing this lifestyle, the self moves off of the throne. Messages are not about self-help; they are about abandonment to God's love in life circumstances. Bible stories aren't taught as a way to make life less messy; they are presented as examples of passionate faith in the midst of the mess. Mario is using his passion for God to impact his acting as he pursues God's best in Hollywood, a rare but necessary mission. Josh, aflame with passion, is freely serving God full-time to significantly impact His generation. Micah, a writer, seeks to turn his passion into non-threatening written works that will grab the imagination of both the seeker and the sold-out believer.

This generation has perhaps more potential than ever before to impact the culture. Anthony Campolo states that youth was never made for pleasure (which is what the culture teaches), but that God made youth for heroism. We remind our people weekly of their status as heroes. Our hearts long for passion. A relevant church provides not the outlet, but the input, for a life of passion.

ENCOUNTER: Transcending the Material to Engage the Spiritual

An encounter with God is another one of our heart's deep desires, and a relevant church provides such an encounter. More than ever, this generation understands that there is spiritual reality, and they are seeking an encounter with the Holy Other. The culture's best has something to do with mixing together substance and sex and a powerful music experience in certain measures at certain times, hinting that a person can transcend themselves and their worries through sensory overload to encounter something spiritual. (Remember Lenny Kravitz's "Fly Away" video? Great song, but the visual message was about excess.)

Our hearts long to encounter God.

A good church invites, without qualification, such a meeting. A relevant church gets out of the way. For much of recent history, church worship has been equated with performance. "The worship was good tonight," has been viewed as a valid commentary on the singing portion of a church service, with the value centered on how in tune the band was, how well the lead vocalist sang, how pretty the PowerPoint was, and how closely the song selection came to pleasing the one making the remark. True worship is so much bigger—it is a literal encounter with the living God. A relevant church understands this and merely gets out of the way, inviting people to enter into God's presence. The message, the songs, the prayer, everything a church includes in its unofficial and official "service" needs to point beyond itself to the reality that God is always available to be encountered. God is always good. God is always near. We simply provide a safe setting (a bit dark, a bit loud, a bit anonymous) to do business with God.

"A RELEVANT CHURCH UNDERSTANDS THAT WORSHIP IS AN ENCOUNTER WITH THE LIVING GOD AND MERELY GETS OUT OF THE WAY, INVITING PEOPLE TO ENTER INTO GOD'S PRESENCE."

Lisa grabbed me after a service last week and with tears in her eyes said, "I met Him here tonight. When we sang that song at the end, 'It is well with my soul'—it was!" Cameron energetically whooped after the service: "Jesus is so good!" Natalie added, "I prayed to get lost in praise tonight. I got lost in it, and God found me there."

Encountering Him is how we stay afloat amid a culture that is anesthetizing our souls to death. Our hearts long for transcendence. A relevant church provides the unobtrusive setting for an encounter with the Holy.

INTIMACY: Building Relationships in Safe Community

More and more, we realize we all are on a journey, and pilgrims on a journey need community. For identity's sake, for safety's sake, for the sake of comfort in the confusion, for the opportunity to grow, spiritual community is an essential. Christianity requires doing faith and life together.

I have found churches where all that is embraced is a shallow pretense of perfection—that Jesus cleans up all the messiness. Such churches are not only irrelevant; they are to be avoided. The truth is that nobody has arrived; nobody is finished with the process. The illusion of perfection makes this generation uneasy. However, what is indispensable is a community of like-minded individuals who, with common values and common goals, journey together through life, knee-deep in the messiness. What is relevant is having a community with which to refuel your soul, to replenish your appetite for spiritual adventure, to reconnect with the Divine, and to rediscover who you are as God's beloved.

"FOR IDENTITY'S SAKE, FOR SAFETY'S SAKE, FOR THE SAKE OF COMFORT IN THE CONFUSION, FOR THE OPPORTUNITY TO GROW, SPIRITUAL COMMUNITY IS AN ESSENTIAL. CHRISTIANITY REQUIRES DOING FAITH AND LIFE TOGETHER."

Our hearts long for relationships. A relevant church provides a real setting for authentic relationships to develop. At CRAVE, we seek to fulfill God's purposes of fellowship and discipleship within the context of small, safe, committed groups. Our small groups run immediately after our Thursday night service; our discipleship cell groups provide mentor relationships and meet whenever and wherever it is convenient for both mentor and student to meet. We seek intimacy—we seek to be known fully, and loved anyway. A relevant church provides safe relationship building opportunities.

CLARITY: An Authentic Expression of Relevant Truth

We long for clarity. An essential ministry provides truth—unadulterated, empowering, and glory-bringing to God. The number one question that comes up in this generation is the question of direction: What am I supposed to do with my life? God's truth provides so much tangible response to that question, largely related to their passion, their relationships, and their willingness to encounter God. T-Bone (I have no desire to know how this moniker came to be) challenged me yesterday to continue to paint the picture of "How great it is to deny ourselves and pick up the cross and follow Him daily—to experience His life daily. To know His salvation daily!" This is a man who experiences clarity in the context of His commitment to Christ, if not in his personal choice of nicknames.

As a communicator, I seek to share God's truth as it impacts me and directs me in my own journey. I filter God's Word through my personal faith experience. This means being transparent, even when it's uncomfortable, even when I fail. Erwin McManus is a hero who leads out in this style of authentic faith sharing. It is a profound spiritual irony that the more I expose my weaknesses and my utter dependence upon Jesus, the more strength and encouragement gets communicated to CRAVE. Leadership means journeying together arm-in-arm. After sharing about the issue of comparing myself to others, and all of the gross pride and insecurity it reveals that I still have in my life, Seth sent me this: "Hi Mike, I just wanted to tell you how much I appreciated your honesty and openness in sharing with CRAVE last Thursday. Your authenticity is one of the best qualities about you, Mike, and I know we all appreciate that sincerity greatly. The message definitely spoke to me, as it's easy for me to compare myself to others, which is SO wrong. Thanks for your leadership!" Truth presented through transparency empowers and encourages a generation hungry for clarity.

Clarity, intimacy, encounter, and passion ... there is no other place in society for these values to be met than within a relevant church. These are the values through which we process everything we do as a ministry, every purpose we seek to fulfill. As the leader of this ministry, I'm constantly evaluating how our ministry programs affirm our values. CRAVE is purpose-driven in what we do, and value-driven in how we do it.

Finally, we need to face the reality that many churches aren't relevant to our lives in this culture because we have abandoned church en masse. If the cutting edge, creative, seeking, developing, graphically sharp, hypocrisy-radar-equipped eighteen- to thirty-year-olds were all to plug back into church, and be committed enough to step into roles of both serving and leading in their areas of giftedness, then the Church at large would strain, break, and be re-stitched with the threads of being essential.

"IF THE CHURCH HAS BECOME IRRELEVANT (AS IT CERTAINLY HAS IN MANY PLACES), IT IS BECAUSE THIS GENERATION HAS WITHDRAWN FROM THE GRAND DIALOGUE. WE NEED TO RE-ENGAGE."

God has purposed the Church to be the lifeblood of His expression in the world; it exists for His glory, and we are honored to be swept up in a movement one day consummated in worship for eternity. If God values church like I value my bride, then our call is to engage her with the highest and best and most talented parts of ourselves, and to adorn her with every grace and gift we have been given by God. We individually exist to bring Him glory; the Church corporately exists for God's glory, and the more relevant we make her, by tuning our values to the world's deep needs, the more glory is ascribed His name. If the Church has become irrelevant (as it certainly has in many places), it is because this generation has withdrawn from the grand dialogue. We need to re-engage.

Re-engage the Church, and discover an emerging organism that is alive, that sweeps us up into living a life of passionate purpose, and that glorifies the God who established her in the first place.

❝ I DON'T GO TO CHURCH OUT OF OBLIGATION, BUT BECAUSE I DESIRE TO WORSHIP JESUS IN A PLACE THAT IS SET ASIDE FOR HIM, A CONSECRATED SPACE. IT'S VERY DIFFERENT THAN A BIBLE STUDY IN MY LIVING ROOM OR JUST PRAYING IN MY CAR. **❞**

—EMILY R. GEYER
MIAMI, FLORIDA, AGE TWENTY-ONE

ABOUT THE AUTHORS

DUSTIN BAGBY is a rock show-a-holic who truly has a desire to be a rock star chaplain. Right now, you will find Death Cab for Cutie, Pedro the Lion, and anything by Ryan Adams playing most heavily on his iPod. You can catch him doing stand-up comedy on the weekends at Gotham Comedy Club in Manhattan. Dustin is a church planting resident with Mosaic Manhattan, a new church in Lower Manhattan, New York, who is trying to engage culture by means of sharing good news through the arts.

SANDRA BARRETT's heart beats to see people come to Christ. Since the mid-'90s, Sandra has watched SKATECHURCH grow from a few youth leaders organizing skate trips to its current eleven thousand square foot warehouse. Previously a missionary with Wycliffe Bible Translators, Sandra now works for the Luis Palau Evangelistic Association in Portland, Oregon, and is committed to the emergence of the experimental church. She's currently hooked on bluegrass, hazelnut lattes, and marionberry muffins.

MIKE BICKLE is the author of *Passion for Jesus, Growing in the Prophetic, The Pleasures of Loving God,* and *After God's Own Heart.* He directs the International House of Prayer of Kansas City, a twenty-four-hour-a-day intercession ministry, and is also the president of Forerunner School of Ministry, a full-time Bible school in Kansas City, Missouri.

MARK DRISCOLL is the founding pastor of Mars Hill Church in Seattle, Washington—one of America's least churched cities. Mark has an M.A. in Exegetical Theology and is the author of *The Radical Reformission: Reaching Out Without Selling Out.* Mark is five-foot-nine-inches, the same height as Jesus, and drives a 1978 Chevy truck with a bacon air freshener. A very long-winded old school Bible thumper who draws from the deep wells of the great preachers Charles Spurgeon and Chris Rock, Mark's sermons can be found free at the church website (*www.marshillchurch.org*), along with live recordings of the church's worship music.

generation. He currently serves at Saddleback Church in Southern California as the college pastor, where he spends his time loving on people who are far hipper and smarter than he is. He lives in the OC with his ultra-cool wife Jodie, angel-sweet daughter Alex, and roaring-bear-cub son Caleb.

BRIAN KAY is known for his ability to recite on command every lyric by The Violent Femmes and for his impeccable impression of Michael Jackson's "Thriller" (both of which embarrass and baffle his friends to no extent). A hardcore Calvinist who loves church history, Brian also teaches in the philosophy department at Cal Poly San Luis Obispo. After receiving his Masters of Divinity from Gordon Conwell, he started Trinity Presbyterian Church in San Luis Obispo, California, in 1996 as a PCA church plant. And thankfully—the event that ended his streak of owning absurd pets—his wife Sally just gave birth to their first baby girl, Willa.

TIM KEEL is the founding pastor of Jacob's Well Church in the midtown community of Kansas City, Missouri. He has been married to Mimi for thirteen years and is the father of Mabry (ten), Annelise (seven), and Blaise (three). Tim graduated from the University of Kansas with a Bachelor of Fine Arts in illustration and received a Masters of Divinity with honors from Denver Seminary. A senior fellow with Emergent (*www.emergentvillage.org*), Tim is passionate about cultivating spaces where people can encounter God, themselves, and others and developing rhythms that are creative and life-giving for individuals and communities. His interests include monastic life and culture, reading, writing, and all things Middle-Earth.

TOMMY KYLLONEN, a.k.a. Urban D., founded the youth ministry at Crossover Community Church in Miami, Florida, in 1996. In 2002 he became the pastor, and the church as a whole began focusing on reaching the hip-hop culture. The church has more than tripled in size and now reaches more than five hundred people weekly on a weekly basis. He has also recorded five solo albums and traveled across the U.S., Germany, and Japan, performing, preaching, and speaking at conferences.

ALEX MCMANUS creates experiences that call the latent spiritual potential within believers and non-believers alike in Los Angeles, California. Whether writing music with his world music band NIZA, leading a team on an eco-adventure, or guiding a group of cross-cultural world-changers to Brazil, Alex seeks to help others develop skills for navigating today's fast moving culture. On the home front, Alex is married to Adriana, whom he met on an expedition to Brazil. They have three children, Michael, Erica, and Lucas. Alex currently serves as a cultural architect and navigator on the Mosaic-lead team in Los Angeles and also oversees Mosaic's International Mission efforts.

IAN NICHOLSON is a Brit with a deep love for Europe—not a common combination! A senior pastor in the South of England, he is passionate about town-wide church unity, mission, new expressions of church, and releasing younger people to dream and initiate. He also directs the mission development of the 24-7 Prayer movement. Past incarnations have seen him as Bible smuggler, TV salesman, and youth worker, but now, quite a bit older and grayer than most of the 24-7 community, Ian gets dragged out to show there are some grown-ups in the building. Crazy about sports, he watches soccer, rugby, and cricket from the safety of his armchair, and his only other addiction is the TV show *24*. Ian has a Bachelor of Arts in sociology and geography, which has been really useful for Trivial Pursuit.

MARK SCANDRETTE is President of Re/IMAGINE, a San Francisco-based organization that fuels initiatives integrating spiritual formation, community making, the arts and social action. He is also director of THE BOON PROJECT, a collective of activist artists associated with Re/IMAGINE. He also serves as Director and Pastor at Lakeside Ministry Center in Oakland, where he is helping create a church community with second generation Southeast Asian-American college students, young-adults and senior citizens. Mark has a B.S. in Applied Psychology, studied at Bethel Theological Seminary in St. Paul and has been a minister, writer and lecturer for eight years. A dilettante poet and painter, Mark lives with his wife Lisa and their three children, Hailey, Noah and Isaiah in an old Victorian in the Mission District of San Francisco.

TODD SPITZER is married to Robyn and has a daughter, Sarai. He grew up eating cheese in Wisconsin and then relocated to New Mexico where he had a pastoral internship at Calvary of Albuquerque. He later joined Cornerstone Fellowship in Livermore, California where he served as a staff pastor. During this time with Cornerstone, he started a Bible study which would grow to become Regeneration. When he's not busy doing the pastor thing, you'll find Todd taking moonlit walks on the beach or curling up by the fireplace with a good book and a cup of Peet's coffee.

KAREN WARD is a blogger, Mac geek, film buff, and fan of idm, glitch, electro, and live p.a. music. Like many Seattleites, she enjoys a good bean- or leaf-based beverage and can often be found dreaming of how a new heaven and a new earth come into praxis at Living:room, the 'net café, tea lounge, and art house of Church of the Apostles in the Fremont neighborhood of Seattle, Washington. Apostles is an Episcopal/Lutheran missional community of which Karen is the pastor.

JASON ZAHARIADES recently left professional ministry in order to pursue his dream of being part of a small missional community called Community of Faith in San Dimas, California. Married with four kids, Jason enjoys dates with his wife, watching good movies, reading theology books, and tinkering with writing. Jason has a Master of Arts in theology from Fuller Theological Seminary.

HOLLY RANKIN ZAHER is currently obsessed with listening to Lori Chaffer and East Mountain South and drinking copious amounts of ginger ale since she's pregnant with her first child. She fumbles with a group of artists at THREENAILS in Pittsburgh, Pennsylvania, as they create their worship gatherings and is an adjunct professor at the Trinity Episcopal School for Ministry (*www.tesm.edu*). Also on Emergent's coordinating group (*www.emergentvillage.org*) and part of Rock the World Youth Mission Alliance (*www.rocktheworld.org*), Holly has a Masters of Divinity, and her writing has appeared in *The Post-Evangelical*.

JENNY ASHLEY has a Masters of Arts in creative writing, and her work has appeared in *Mars Hill Review*, *Re:Generation Quarterly*, *RELEVANT* magazine, *Oxford* magazine, *The Allegheny Review*, *I AM RELEVANT*, and other publications. She works as an editor, writer, and English instructor in San Luis Obispo, California. On a journey to unite her reliance on Christ with her passion for writing, Jenny also co-leads "Art Project: An Ongoing Discussion of Art, Faith and Culture" at Trinity Presbyterian Church in San Luis Obispo, where she and her goofball husband Charles are members.

ABOUT THE CHURCHES

MOSAIC MANHATTAN is a new Christian Church in Lower Manhattan that began in March of 2003. Mosaic draws a diverse mix of around 175 people, ranging from video editors, tattoo artists, dancers, comedians, students, and businessmen and women, to everything in between. They especially welcome those who have never been to church or who have been burned by the Church in the past. They understand that many people in New York City have a negative connotation of what church and Christianity is, so they are inviting people to help them redefine church in their lives and in that community.

SKATECHURCH is a place where young people come on a daily basis to find good ramps and God. In the intense Northwest skate culture of Portland, Skatechurch is in essence a warehouse with the best ramps in the city. A great place to get out of the rain, hang out with people your age, and get in some good runs, there's also a set time in each session when everyone gathers at the bleachers to hear Paul Anderson talk for thirty minutes about Christ straight from the Bible. Since Skatechurch was built in 1996, more than ten thousand young people have been introduced to the message of Christ, and more than one thousand have come to believe in Him. For the countless who encountered Jesus just by skating and listening, there's also a Saturday night service that draws an intergenerational mix of fellow skaters, college students, and young professionals each weekend.

MARS HILL CHURCH is in the heart of eccentric downtown Seattle, the most unchurched urban center in the nation. Since its inception in 1996, Mars Hill has grown from a twelve-person Bible study to more than two thousand people who attend weekly, solely by word of mouth. Their forty-thousand square foot warehouse bustles with people of all ages, from an excessive amount of young hipsters in their twenties and thirties to larger families and grandparents. Often looked to as one of the leading experimental churches, Mars Hill influenced many others in the late '90s to embrace culture into order to impact culture by incorporating modern and contemporary art, mystic candlelight, as well as indie-rock music in their services. Mars Hill runs the all ages concert and music venue Paradox Theater—one of the best places to see an all-ages punk show in Seattle—as well as Acts 29, an organization that has planted one hundred churches in eight countries in the last ten years.

SADDLEBACK CHURCH is a dynamically active purpose-driven church in Lake Forest, California, and weekly serves more than twenty thousand men, women, and children (they'd count pets, too, if you brought yours). SIX is the name of their service geared toward reaching the emerging suburban generation, which draws more than fifteen hundred worshippers. CRAVE, the college age ministry, currently serves more than five hundred eighteen- to twenty-four-year-olds. The purposes Saddleback seeks to fulfill are found in the Word, and are: evangelism, fellowship, discipleship, ministry, and worship; and it's all done on purpose, and it's all for God's glory.

TRINITY PRESBYTERIAN CHURCH is a community of thinkers, believers, and regularly-attending skeptics. Meeting in Oddfellows Hall in San Luis Obispo, California, since 1995, the church has a low-tech feel (acoustic guitar for contemporary worship plus a few hymns) that draws an intergenerational mix of one hundred and fifty academics, scientists, college students, and many twenty- and thirty-something newly marrieds and never-marrieds. Trinity's service is steeped in ancient tradition (reciting corporate creeds and confessions, as well as taking communion with real wine), and each ritual is continually made relevant by explaining its origin, meaning, and importance in contemporary life. People who frequent Trinity Pres on Sundays also gather during the week for Bible studies, theology classes, guitar workshops, book and movie discussions, and more.

MOSAIC: LOS ANGELES. Lights stream through a nightclub as hundreds of young Asians, whites, and Latinos dance and clap to the music. The room pulses with energy, and then a hush sets in as Erwin McManus perches on a stool to talk about three symbols of death—the cross, baptism, and the Lord's Supper. This is Mosaic, a creative arts church fueled by single twentysomethings from downtown Los Angeles. Meeting in a nightclub that formerly belonged to Prince, Mosaic's name comes from its diversity, but also from the symbolism of broken humanity that God forms into a work of beauty.

THE FIRST 24-7 PRAYER ROOM began in the U.K. in September 1999 when a small community of students and young people prayed nonstop for three months for God to "turn the tide" in youth culture. The virus has since spread to fifty-two nations and more than twenty-two hundred prayer weeks. 24-7 rooms are creative, interactive, and highly visual prayer spaces that inspire and connect well with emerging culture. Many of the community members have been at the forefront in experimenting with new models of "non-religious" church, the use of dance, DJs, and bands in worship, and new expressions of incarnational, grassroots mission in youth culture. Some 24-7 rooms are integrated within existing churches, others help build partnerships between churches in towns, while other "boiler rooms" are being developed from scratch. Boiler rooms are intentional and committed communities with values of prayer, mission, justice, pilgrimage, and creativity at the core. The 24-7 movement is also linked with an interactive website, *www.24-7prayer.com*.

COMMUNITY OF FAITH, San Dimas, began in May of 2003. It is a small community of friends who come together frequently in a home with the sole intention of spurring one another on to become authentic apprentices of Jesus. "Official" meetings consist of a weekly formation meeting, bi-weekly accountability groups, and a bi-weekly common meal and worship (although a lot of cool relational stuff happens "behind the scenes"). Their official website and members' blogs can be found at *www.theofframp.org*.

CROSSOVER COMMUNITY CHURCH in Tampa, Florida, was established in 1991. Tommy Kyllonen founded the youth ministry in 1996 and became the pastor in 2002. Crossover has become known as the first hip-hop church in the world, as it uses music and elements of the culture. The church reaches a multi-cultural crowd that is made up of more than five hundred predominately younger urban adults and families.

CHURCH OF THE APOSTLES is an emerging missional community in Seattle seeking to bring future expression to the ancient Christian faith. A young church (average age twenty-six), Apostles is part of the Episcopal and Lutheran tribes and meets at living:room, a net lounge and tea bar in Seattle's Fremont neighborhood. All sojourners are welcome. *www.apostleschurch.org*

JACOB'S WELL CHURCH is a community of people seeking to live authentically and biblically in the way of Jesus. Gathering in an old Presbyterian church in the midtown community of Kansas City, Missouri, Jacob's Well is filled with a broad array of people who are exploring what it means to experience and express the reality of God's love in the context of our neighborhoods, our city, and our world. Tim Keel graciously invites you to come and participate.

THREENAILS desires to be a movement of people who are following Jesus. Commissioned by the Episcopal Diocese of Pittsburgh to begin a new form of church planting specifically for a younger generation, THREENAILS is now home to people from ages 2 to 60 who desire church to be descriptive of a group of people rather than a building or a program. THREENAILS, which began in 2003, exists to see a contagious release of God's freedom and purpose in the world.

REGENERATION hosts an eclectic mix of people who are digging deep the ancient wells of Scripture to discover the person of Jesus. Todd Spitzer invites you to be a part of their community in the East Bay on Sunday nights and in San Francisco,s Mission District for gatherings mid-week. *www.regenerationweb.com*

THE PLAYERS

DUSTIN BAGBY
Mosaic Manhattan
New York, NY
www.mosaicmanhattan.com

MIKE HOWERTON
Saddleback Community
Lake Forest, CA
www.saddleback.com

SANDRA BARRETT
SKATECHURCH
Portland, OR
www.skatechurch.net

BRIAN KAY
Trinity Presbyterian Church
San Luis Obispo, CA
www.trinityslo.org

MIKE BICKLE
International House of Prayer
Kansas City, MO
www.fotb.com

TIM KEEL
Jacob's Well
Kansas City, MO
www.jacobswellchurch.org

MARK DRISCOLL
Mars Hill Church
Seattle, WA
www.marshillchurch.org

**TOMMY KYLLONEN
(URBAN D.)**
Crossover Community
Tampa, FL
www.flavoralliance.com

ALEX MCMANUS
Mosaic
Los Angeles, CA
www.mosaic.org

KAREN WARD
Church of the Apostles
Seattle, WA
www.apostleschurch.org

IAN NICHOLSON
24-7 prayer
www.24-7prayer.com

JASON ZAHARIADES
Community of Faith
San Dimas, CA
www.theofframp.org

MARK SCANDRETTE
Re:Imagine!
San Francisco, CA
www.emergentvillage.com

HOLLY ZAHER
THREENAILS
Pittsburgh, PA
http://threenails.org

TODD SPITZER
Regeneration
Berkeley, CA
www.regenerationweb.com

PHOTO CREDITS

Jenny Ashley, photo by Kellian Ehrheart
Dustin Bagby, photo by Deborah Fischer
Sandra Barrett, photo by Katie Jones
Mike Bickle, photo by Elizabeth Peterson
Mark Driscoll, photo by Thomas James Hurst
Mike Howerton, photo by Jim Dobbs
Tim Keel, photo by Timothy Keel
Tommy Kyllonen (a.k.a. Urban D.) photo by Spec of FlavorDezigns
Brian Kay, photo by Sally Pinkerton Kay
Alex McManus, photo by Tammy Borrerro
Ian Nicholson, photo provided by 24-7prayer.com
Mark Scandrette, photo by Michael Toy
Todd Spitzer, photo by John Mockus
Holly Rankin Zaher, photo by David Sadd
Karen Ward, photo by Ryan Marsh
Jason Zahariades, photo by Mark Feliciano

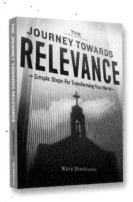